Elements of Literature

First Course

Holt Adapted Reader

from *Elements of Literature*
- Adapted Literary Selections
- Poetry Selections
- Adapted Informational Texts

HOLT, RINEHART AND WINSTON

A Harcourt Education Company

Orlando • **Austin** • New York • San Diego • Toronto • London

CREDITS

Executive Editor: Katie Vignery

Senior Editor: Amy Strong

Editor: Nicole Svobodny

Copyediting: Michael Neibergall, *Copyediting Manager;* Kristen Azzara, Mary Malone, *Copyediting Supervisors;* Christine Altgelt, Elizabeth Dickson, Leora Harris, Anne Heausler, Kathleen Scheiner, *Senior Copyeditors;* Emily Force, Julia Thomas Hu, Nancy Shore, *Copyeditors*

Project Administration: Marie Price, *Managing Editor;* Elizabeth LaManna, *Associate Managing Editor;* Janet Jenkins, *Senior Editorial Coordinator;* Christine Degollado, Betty Gabriel, Mark Koenig, Erik Netcher, *Editorial Coordinators*

Permissions: Ann Farrar, *Senior Permissions Editor;* Sally Garland, Susan Lowrance, *Permissions Editors*

Design: Richard Metzger, Betty Mintz

Production: Beth Prevelige, *Senior Production Manager;* Carol Trammel, *Production Manager;* Leanna Ford, Belinda Barbosa Lopez, Michael Roche, *Senior Production Coordinators;* Dolores Keller, Carol Marunas, *Production Coordinators;* Myles Gorospe, *Production Assistant*

Publishing Services: Laura Likon, *Technical Services Director;* Juan Baquera, *Technical Services Manager;* Margaret Sanchez, *Senior Technical Services Analyst*

Manufacturing: Shirley Cantrell, *Manufacturing Supervisor;* Mark McDonald, *Inventory Analyst;* Amy Borseth, *Manufacturing Coordinator*

Printed in the United States of America

ISBN 0-03-035711-X

1 2 3 4 5 6   179   04 03

Contents

Reading Literature

Skills Table of Contents

Reading Skills

Literary Skills

Vocabulary Skills

To the Student

A Book for You

Imagine this. A book full of great stories and interesting informational articles. Make it a book that actually tells you to write in it. Fill it with graphic organizers that encourage you to think a different way. Make it a size that's easy to carry around. That's *Holt Adapted Reader*—a book created especially for you.

In *Holt Adapted Reader*, you will find two kinds of selections— adaptations and original selections.

Adaptations are based on stories or articles that appear in *Elements of Literature*, First Course. Adaptations make the selections more accessible to all readers. You can easily identify any selection that is an adaptation. Just look for the words "based on" in the Table of Contents or selection opener.

Some adaptations in this booklet begin with a feature called **YOU NEED TO KNOW**. This feature provides background information required to understand the selection.

Original selections are exactly as they appear in *Elements of Literature*, First Course. The poem in this book is an example of an original selection. As you read original selections, you will find helps called **IN OTHER WORDS**. In Other Words paraphrases the text that comes before it. That is, it restates the text in different words.

Learning to Read Literary and Informational Texts

When you read informational texts like a social studies textbook or a newspaper article, you usually read to get the facts. You read mainly to get information that is stated directly on the page. When you read literature, you need to go beyond the words on the page. You need to read between the lines of a poem or story to discover the writer's meaning. No matter what kind of reading you do, *Holt Adapted Reader* will help you practice the skills and strategies you need to become an active and successful reader.

A Walk Through

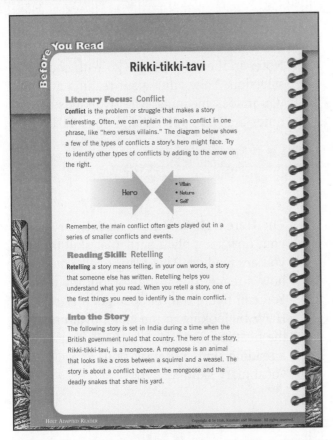

Before You Read

The Before You Read page previews the skill or skills you will practice as you read the selection.

- In the **Literary Focus**, you will learn about one literary element—like character or rhyme. This literary element is one you will see in the selection.
- The **Reading Skill** presents a key skill you will need to read the selection.

The Before You Read page also introduces you to the reading selection.

- **Into the Story** (or Poem, or Article) gives you background information. This information will help you understand the selection or its author. It may also help you understand the time period in which the selection was written.

Interactive Selections from *Elements of Literature*

The readings are many of the same ones that appear in *Elements of Literature*, First Course. Most selections are adaptations. A few are the original selections. The selections are reprinted in a single column and in larger type. This gives you the room you need to mark up the text.

A Walk Through

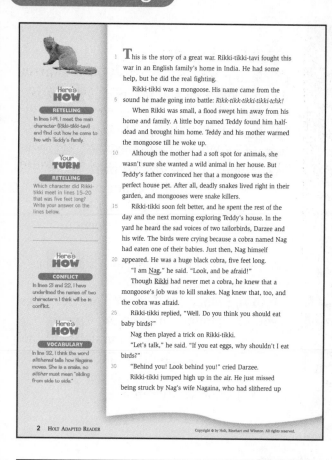

1 This is the story of a great war. Rikki-tikki-tavi fought this war in an English family's home in India. He had some help, but he did the real fighting.

Rikki-tikki was a mongoose. His name came from the 5 sound he made going into battle: *Rikki-tikki-tikki-tchk!*

When Rikki was small, a flood swept him away from his home and family. A little boy named Teddy found him half-dead and brought him home. Teddy and his mother warmed the mongoose till he woke up.

10 Although the mother had a soft spot for animals, she wasn't sure she wanted a wild animal in her house. But Teddy's father convinced her that a mongoose was the perfect house pet. After all, deadly snakes lived right in their garden, and mongooses were snake killers.

15 Rikki-tikki soon felt better, and he spent the rest of the day and the next morning exploring Teddy's house. In the yard he heard the sad voices of two tailorbirds, Darzee and his wife. The birds were crying because a cobra named Nag had eaten one of their babies. Just then, Nag himself 20 appeared. He was a huge black cobra, five feet long.

"I am <u>Nag</u>," he said. "Look, and be afraid!"

Though <u>Rikki</u> had never met a cobra, he knew that a mongoose's job was to kill snakes. Nag knew that, too, and the cobra was afraid.

25 Rikki-tikki replied, "Well. Do you think you should eat baby birds?"

Nag then played a trick on Rikki-tikki.

"Let's talk," he said. "If you eat eggs, why shouldn't I eat birds?"

30 "Behind you! Look behind you!" cried Darzee.

Rikki-tikki jumped high up in the air. He just missed being struck by Nag's wife Nagaina, who had slithered up

---

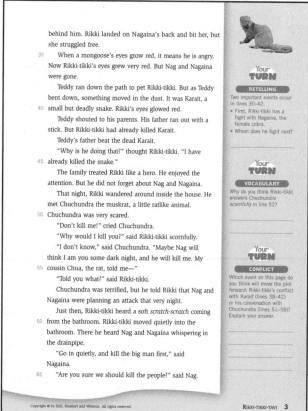

behind him. Rikki landed on Nagaina's back and bit her, but she struggled free.

35 When a mongoose's eyes grow red, it means he is angry. Now Rikki-tikki's eyes grew very red. But Nag and Nagaina were gone.

Teddy ran down the path to pet Rikki-tikki. But as Teddy bent down, something moved in the dust. It was Karait, a 40 small but deadly snake. Rikki's eyes glowed red.

Teddy shouted to his parents. His father ran out with a stick. But Rikki-tikki had already killed Karait.

Teddy's father beat the dead Karait.

"Why is he doing that?" thought Rikki-tikki. "I have 45 already killed the snake."

The family treated Rikki like a hero. He enjoyed the attention. But he did not forget about Nag and Nagaina.

That night, Rikki wandered around inside the house. He met Chuchundra the muskrat, a little ratlike animal. 50 Chuchundra was very scared.

"Don't kill me!" cried Chuchundra.

"Why would I kill you?" said Rikki-tikki scornfully.

"I don't know," said Chuchundra. "Maybe Nag will think I am you some dark night, and he will kill me. My 55 cousin Chua, the rat, told me—"

"Told you what?" said Rikki-tikki.

Chuchundra was terrified, but he told Rikki that Nag and Nagaina were planning an attack that very night.

Just then, Rikki-tikki heard a soft *scratch-scratch* coming 60 from the bathroom. Rikki-tikki moved quietly into the bathroom. There he heard Nag and Nagaina whispering in the drainpipe.

"Go in quietly, and kill the big man first," said Nagaina.

65 "Are you sure we should kill the people?" said Nag.

Side Notes

Notes in the side column go with each selection. They guide your reading and help you unlock meaning. The two kinds of notes are **Here's HOW** and **Your TURN**.

The **Here's HOW** feature models, or shows you, how to apply a particular skill to what you are reading. This feature lets you see how a reader might think about the text. You can figure out the focus of a Here's HOW by looking in the green oval under the heading. Each Here's HOW focuses on a reading skill, a literary skill, or a vocabulary skill.

The **Your TURN** feature gives you a chance to practice a skill on your own. Each Your TURN focuses on a reading skill, a literary skill, or a vocabulary skill. You might be asked to underline or circle words in the text. You might also be asked to write your response on lines that are provided for you.

A Walk Through

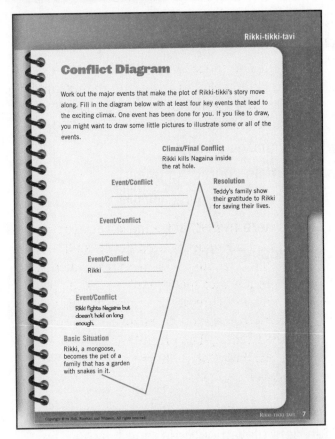

Graphic Organizers

After each selection is a **graphic organizer.** These organizers give you another way to understand the reading or literary focus of the selection. For example, you might be asked to chart the main events of the plot. Or you could be asked to complete a cause-and-effect chain.

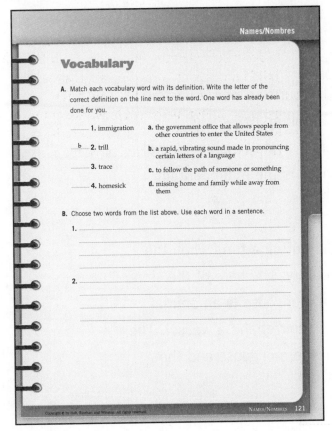

Vocabulary

Some selections have **vocabulary** worksheets at the end. These worksheets help you learn new words. Sometimes you'll learn new meanings for words you already know.

Rikki-tikki-tavi

Literary Focus: Conflict

Conflict is the problem or struggle that makes a story interesting. Often, we can explain the main conflict in one phrase, like "hero versus villains." The diagram below shows a few of the types of conflicts a story's hero might face. Try to identify other types of conflicts by adding to the arrow on the right.

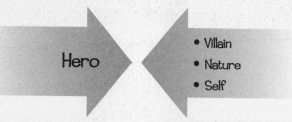

Hero

- Villain
- Nature
- Self

Remember, the main conflict often gets played out in a series of smaller conflicts and events.

Reading Skill: Retelling

Retelling a story means telling, in your own words, a story that someone else has written. Retelling helps you understand what you read. When you retell a story, one of the first things you need to identify is the main conflict.

Into the Story

The following story is set in India during a time when the British government ruled that country. The hero of the story, Rikki-tikki-tavi, is a mongoose. A mongoose is an animal that looks like a cross between a squirrel and a weasel. The story is about a conflict between the mongoose and the deadly snakes that share his yard.

Rikki-tikki-tavi

Based on the Story by

Rudyard Kipling

RETELLING

In lines 1–14, I meet the main character (Rikki-tikki-tavi) and find out how he came to live with Teddy's family.

RETELLING

Which character did Rikki-tikki meet in lines 15–20 that was five feet long? Write your answer on the lines below.

_____

_____

CONFLICT

In lines 21 and 22, I have underlined the names of two characters I think will be in conflict.

VOCABULARY

In line 32, I think the word _slithered_ tells how Nagaina moves. She is a snake, so _slither_ must mean "sliding from side to side."

1   This is the story of a great war. Rikki-tikki-tavi fought this war in an English family's home in India. He had some help, but he did the real fighting.

Rikki-tikki was a mongoose. His name came from the
5   sound he made going into battle: *Rikk-tikk-tikki-tikki-tchk!*

When Rikki was small, a flood swept him away from his home and family. A little boy named Teddy found him half-dead and brought him home. Teddy and his mother warmed the mongoose till he woke up.

10   Although the mother had a soft spot for animals, she wasn't sure she wanted a wild animal in her house. But Teddy's father convinced her that a mongoose was the perfect house pet. After all, deadly snakes lived right in their garden, and mongooses were snake killers.

15   Rikki-tikki soon felt better, and he spent the rest of the day and the next morning exploring Teddy's house. In the yard he heard the sad voices of two tailorbirds, Darzee and his wife. The birds were crying because a cobra named Nag had eaten one of their babies. Just then, Nag himself
20   appeared. He was a huge black cobra, five feet long.

"I am <u>Nag</u>," he said. "Look, and be afraid!"

Though <u>Rikki</u> had never met a cobra, he knew that a mongoose's job was to kill snakes. Nag knew that, too, and the cobra was afraid.

25   Rikki-tikki replied, "Well. Do you think you should eat baby birds?"

Nag then played a trick on Rikki-tikki.

"Let's talk," he said. "If you eat eggs, why shouldn't I eat birds?"

30   "Behind you! Look behind you!" cried Darzee.

Rikki-tikki jumped high up in the air. He just missed being struck by Nag's wife Nagaina, who had slithered up

behind him. Rikki landed on Nagaina's back and bit her, but she struggled free.

35   When a mongoose's eyes grow red, it means he is angry. Now Rikki-tikki's eyes grew very red. But Nag and Nagaina were gone.

   Teddy ran down the path to pet Rikki-tikki. But as Teddy bent down, something moved in the dust. It was Karait, a
40 small but deadly snake. Rikki's eyes glowed red.

   Teddy shouted to his parents. His father ran out with a stick. But Rikki-tikki had already killed Karait.

   Teddy's father beat the dead Karait.

   "Why is he doing that?" thought Rikki-tikki. "I have
45 already killed the snake."

   The family treated Rikki like a hero. He enjoyed the attention. But he did not forget about Nag and Nagaina.

   That night, Rikki wandered around inside the house. He met Chuchundra the muskrat, a little ratlike animal.
50 Chuchundra was very scared.

   "Don't kill me!" cried Chuchundra.

   "Why would I kill you?" said Rikki-tikki scornfully.

   "I don't know," said Chuchundra. "Maybe Nag will think I am you some dark night, and he will kill me. My
55 cousin Chua, the rat, told me—"

   "Told you what?" said Rikki-tikki.

   Chuchundra was terrified, but he told Rikki that Nag and Nagaina were planning an attack that very night.

   Just then, Rikki-tikki heard a soft *scratch-scratch* coming
60 from the bathroom. Rikki-tikki moved quietly into the bathroom. There he heard Nag and Nagaina whispering in the drainpipe.

   "Go in quietly, and kill the big man first," said Nagaina.

65   "Are you sure we should kill the people?" said Nag.

RETELLING

Two important events occur in lines 30–42.

- First, Rikki-tikki has a fight with Nagaina, the female cobra.
- Whom does he fight next?

_____

_____

VOCABULARY

Why do you think Rikki-tikki answers Chuchundra *scornfully* in line 52?

_____

_____

_____

Your TURN

CONFLICT

Which event on this page do you think will move the plot forward: Rikki-tikki's conflict with Karait (lines 38–42) or his conversation with Chuchundra (lines 51–58)? Explain your answer.

_____

_____

_____

_____

"Of course. The mongoose will leave if we kill them. Then we can be king and queen of the garden, and we will have a safe hatching ground for our eggs," said Nagaina. She and Nag had eggs that were almost ready to hatch.

70 Nag slipped through the drain into the bathroom. His head came first, then his five feet of scaly body. Rikki-tikki was angry, but also afraid. He stayed very still for an hour. Then, he moved slowly toward Nag. He knew he had to kill Nag with his first bite. Rikki jumped on Nag's head. Nag

75 shook him every which way. Though Rikki was dizzy and hurt all over, he held on tightly.

Then Rikki felt a blast. The fight had awakened Teddy's father, who shot Nag.

The man picked up Rikki. He shouted, "It's the

80 mongoose again! This time, he has saved our lives!"

Exhausted, Rikki-tikki dragged himself to Teddy's bedroom.

When morning came, Rikki-tikki knew he had a job to finish. Nagaina was still alive. Rikki went to Darzee for help.

85 Darzee told Rikki that Nagaina was by the trash heap, crying over Nag's body. Her eggs were in the melon garden. But the foolish Darzee refused to help Rikki get rid of the cobra's eggs. Darzee didn't think it was fair to destroy eggs.

90 Darzee's wife had more common sense. She didn't want young cobras around. She helped Rikki by fluttering around, pretending her wing was broken. Nagaina couldn't resist such an easy target, so she pursued the bird.

Meanwhile, Rikki-tikki found Nagaina's twenty-five soft,

95 white eggs. He had crushed all but one when he heard Darzee's wife screaming:

"Rikki-tikki, I led Nagaina toward the house. Now she is going in! Hurry! She is going to kill!"

Holding the last egg in his mouth, Rikki-tikki hurried to
100 the porch.

There, Teddy and his parents sat at the breakfast table.
They were as still as stones, hardly daring to breathe.
Nagaina was coiled up on the floor by Teddy's chair.

Rikki-tikki came up and cried, "Turn round and fight,
105 Nagaina!"

"I will fight you soon," she said, but she didn't turn away
from Teddy's bare leg.

Rikki-tikki's eyes were blood red. "Look what I have
here," he said. "Your last egg! I have smashed all the
110 others."

Nagaina spun around. Teddy's father grabbed Teddy and
pulled him across the table to safety.

"Tricked! *Rikk-tck-tck!*" laughed Rikki-tikki. *"Rikki-tikki-
tck-tck!* Now, come and fight with me."

115 Nagaina looked at her egg. "Give me the egg, Rikki-tikki.
I will go away and never come back," she said, lowering
her hood.

"Yes, you will go away—to the trash heap. Fight!" said
Rikki-tikki.

120 They circled each other in a deadly dance. But Rikki had
forgotten the egg. Nagaina quickly caught her last egg in her
mouth and raced away with it. Rikki-tikki followed her and
caught her tail in his sharp little teeth. Together they
disappeared down a rat hole.

125 Darzee, who was watching the battle, cried, "A
mongoose has no chance against a snake down there.
Brave Rikki is dead!"

But suddenly, the grass moved again. There was Rikki-
tikki. He dragged himself out of the hole.

130 "It is all over," Rikki said. "Nagaina is dead."

Here's HOW

VOCABULARY

The word *coiled* in line 103 tells how the snake was lying on the floor. I think it means that the snake was lying in a circle. I checked the dictionary, and it says "gathered in loops or circles." My meaning was correct.

Your TURN

RETELLING

- Nagaina offers to leave the yard in exchange for her last egg.
- How does Rikki respond when Nagaina asks Rikki to give her back the egg? The answer lies in lines 115–119.

_____

_____

_____

_____

_____

_____

_____

Your TURN

CONFLICT

The major problem in a story usually gets solved before it ends. Re-read lines 130–142. Put a check next to a line that tells you the conflict is over.

Then he curled up right there and slept until late afternoon. He didn't even hear the Coppersmith, a little bird whose job it was to shout out the good news.

That night at the house, Rikki ate a feast. He was amused
135 by all the fuss.

"Just think, he saved our lives and Teddy's life," said Teddy's mother.

"What are they worried about?" Rikki-tikki wondered. "The cobras are all dead. And if any more come, I'm here."
140 Rikki-tikki was proud in his own way, and he had a right to be. From then on, he protected the yard. No cobra ever again dared to enter it.

Conflict Diagram

Work out the major events that make the plot of Rikki-tikki's story move along. Fill in the diagram below with at least four key events that lead to the exciting climax. One event has been done for you. If you like to draw, you might want to draw some little pictures to illustrate some or all of the events.

Climax/Final Conflict
Rikki kills Nagaina inside the rat hole.

Event/Conflict
_____
_____

Resolution
Teddy's family show their gratitude to Rikki for saving their lives.

Event/Conflict
_____
_____

Event/Conflict
Rikki _____
_____

Event/Conflict
Rikki fights Nagaina but doesn't hold on long enough.

Basic Situation
Rikki, a mongoose, becomes the pet of a family that has a garden with snakes in it.

India's History

Reading Skill: Text Structure

Textbooks are good sources of information. They follow a special structure to help you find that information. This **text structure** is found in most textbooks.

A **table of contents** is found at the front of almost every textbook. The table of contents tells you where to find a certain topic.

You can often find **prereading** features at the beginning of a chapter or selection. These features tell you what to look for when you read. They list main points, key terms, and background information.

Photos and **graphics** make books look good. Maps, charts, and graphs also give you extra information. Each graphic usually has a title or **caption** that describes it.

Some textbooks have prereading **questions** to help you find important points. Questions after each section help you review important points.

Into the Textbook

The next few pages are from a geography textbook. The title of the book is *People, Places, and Change.* See how well you understand the structure of the textbook.

INDIA'S HISTORY **9**

Here's HOW

TEXT STRUCTURE

What's Unit 9 about? South Asia. I'm not sure where that is. Two lines below, it says "Atlas." I think that means we're going to see some maps. Maybe the maps will show exactly what countries are in this unit. Next is "Fast Facts." That probably will be some information about how many people live there. Here we go: Chapter 30 is about India. Hey, wasn't the story "Rikki-tikki-tavi" set in India?

Your TURN

TEXT STRUCTURE

The **table of contents** is an important part of a textbook. What major topics on India does this textbook cover?

_____

_____

_____

_____

_____

_____

Section 2 India's History

Reading Focus

- What outside groups affected India's history?
- What was the Mughal Empire like?
- How did Great Britain gain control of India?
- Why was India divided when it became independent?

Key Terms
Sanskrit
sepoys
boycott

Key Places
Delhi
Calcutta
Mumbai

Coat of arms of the East India Company

You Be the Geographer

India has been invaded several times by outside groups. These groups added new customs and beliefs to India's diverse culture. Besides through invasion, how do ideas spread from country to country?

Early Indian Civilizations

Mohenjo Daro was one of the largest cities of the Harappan civilization.

Interpreting the Visual Record How might you tell from this photo that Harappan cities were well planned?

▼

The first civilization on the Indian subcontinent was centered around the Indus River valley. Its territory was mainly in present-day Pakistan but also extended into India. Scholars call this the Harappan civilization after one of its cities, Harappa. By about 2500 B.C. the people of this civilization were living in large, well-planned cities. Scholars believe the Harappans traded with the peoples of Mesopotamia. The Harappans had a system of writing, but scholars have not been able to read it. Very little is known about Harappan religion and customs.

The Taj Mahal is one of the most famous buildings in the world.

The British

Movement During the 1700s and 1800s the British slowly took control of India. At first this was done by the English East India Company. This company won rights to trade in the Mughal Empire in the 1600s. The East India Company first took control of small trading posts. Later the British gained more Indian territory.

Company Rule As the Mughal Empire grew weaker, the English East India Company expanded its political power. The company also built up its own military force. This army was made up mostly of **sepoys**, Indian troops commanded by British officers. The British used the strategy of backing one Indian ruler against another in exchange for cooperation. By the mid-1800s the company controlled more than half of India. The rest was divided into small states ruled by local princes.

The British changed the Indian economy to benefit British industry. India produced raw materials, including cotton, indigo—a natural dye—and jute. These materials were then shipped to Britain for use in British factories. Spices, sugar, tea, and wheat were also grown in India for export. Railroads were built to ship the raw materials to Calcutta, Bombay (now Mumbai), and other port cities. India also became a market for British manufactured goods. Indians, who had woven cotton cloth for centuries, were now forced to buy British cloth.

In September 1857, British and loyal Sikh troops stormed the gate of Delhi, defended by rebel sepoys. Bloody fighting continued until late 1858.

Interpreting the Visual Record
How did the Indian Mutiny lead to a change in the way India was governed?

India • 657

Your TURN

TEXT STRUCTURE

The **caption** says that the Taj Mahal is a famous building. The teacher said the building is in Agra, India. The **inset** map shows where Agra is in India. In what part of India is the Taj Mahal?

Here's HOW

TEXT STRUCTURE

Key parts of a chapter are set as heads. The type is usually boldface, large, and sometimes in color. Key ideas and terms are set in boldface type, too. I know "The British" is an important part of this section because it is a boldface head.

Your TURN

TEXT STRUCTURE

Key terms are often set in **boldface type.** Often, these terms are defined in the text. Circle the boldface word and underline its meaning.

TEXT STRUCTURE

Often, textbooks have little reviews and reading checks. They let me know if I'm getting the main points or if I need to re-read. They also help me remember what I've read. The questions they ask show me what's important. Sometimes, the teacher puts those questions on our tests.

Your
TURN

TEXT STRUCTURE

Circle the second **Reading Check** and circle the section of text where you would find the answer to the question.

Your
TURN

TEXT STRUCTURE

Questions usually end each section. These questions help you review what you've read. If you can't answer the questions, you need to re-read the text. Using the information in the text, answer question 3 on the lines below.

_____

_____

_____

_____

Anti-British Protest

After World War I more and more Indians began demanding the end of British rule. A lawyer named Mohandas K. Gandhi became the most important leader of this Indian independence movement.

Gandhi and Nonviolence *Place* Gandhi reached out to the millions of Indian peasants. He used a strategy of nonviolent mass protest. He called for Indians to peacefully refuse to cooperate with the British. Gandhi led protest marches and urged Indians to **boycott**, or refuse to buy, British goods. Many times the police used violence against marchers. When the British jailed Gandhi, he went on hunger strikes. Gandhi's determination and self-sacrifice attracted many followers. Pressure grew on Britain to leave India.

✔ **READING CHECK:** Do you know how India came under British control?

Independence and Division

Region After World War II the British government decided to give India independence. The British government and the Indian National Congress wanted India to become one country. However, India's Muslims demanded a separate Muslim state. Anger and fear grew between Hindus and Muslims. India seemed on the verge of civil war.

Finally, in 1947 the British divided their Indian colony into two independent countries, India and Pakistan. India was mostly Hindu. Pakistan, which then included what is today Bangladesh, was mostly Muslim. However, the new boundary left millions of Hindus in Pakistan and millions of Muslims in India. Masses of people rushed to cross the border. Hundreds of thousands were killed in rioting and panic.

✔ **READING CHECK:** Do you know why India was divided when it became independent?

▲
Mohandas Gandhi was known to his followers as the Mahatma, or the "great soul."

Section Review 2

Define Sanskrit, sepoys, boycott

Working with Sketch Maps On the map you created in Section 1, label Delhi, Calcutta, and Mumbai. What bodies of water are important to each of these cities?

Reading for Content Understanding

1. *Region* What factors made the Mughal Empire one of the most powerful states in the world?

2. *Movement* How did the English East India Company gain control of most of India?

3. *Place* Who was the most important leader of the Indian independence movement, and what was his strategy?

You Be the Geographer: CRITICAL THINKING

4. *Movement* Why was the British colony of India divided into two countries?

Organizing What You Know

5. Copy the following time line. Use it to mark important events in Indian history from 2500 B.C. to A.D. 1947.

2500 B.C. ———————————— A.D. 1947

Reading Check

Use the textbook pages you just read to answer the following questions.
The last question has been answered for you.

1. According to the **Table of Contents,** what chapters are covered in
   Unit 9?

   _____

   _____

   _____

2. Which part of the **Table of Contents** is covered in the text that you
   read? List the chapter and section numbers.

   _____

   _____

   _____

3. What do the **Reading Focus** questions tell you about the text before
   you read it?

   _____

   _____

   _____

4. Use the **boldface heads** to list the main topics about India's history
   that the text covers.

   _____

   _____

   _____

5. Why are some words in **boldface** type?
   They are key terms.

   _____

Three Skeleton Key

Literary Focus: Suspense and Foreshadowing

Do you ever sit on the edge of your chair in a movie theater, worrying what will happen next? Maybe you wonder, "What's behind the door? Is she going to open the door?" Then you scream out, "Don't open the door!" This feeling of nervous curiosity is called **suspense.**

Writers often build suspense by dropping clues about what may happen later in the story. This use of clues is called **foreshadowing.** For example: First, a character hears a noise. Then, the character looks at a door. Then, the character walks slowly to the door.

Reading Skill: Making Predictions

When you try to guess what will happen next, you are **making a prediction.** Don't worry if your prediction isn't correct. After all, if you could guess everything that happens in a story before it happens, you'd get bored. Clever writers will often surprise you.

Into the Story

Are you ready? You're about to read a very scary story. As you read, look for clues that foreshadow something that will happen. As the suspense builds, try to predict possible outcomes. Stay calm, and watch out for the rats!

Three Skeleton Key

BASED ON THE STORY BY
George G. Toudouze

YOU NEED TO KNOW The title of this story is the name of a key, or low-lying island. This island is located off the coast of French Guiana (gee AHN eh) in South America.

1 What was my most terrifying experience? Well, working in a lighthouse is mostly quite boring. You have to keep the light in order and write reports. However, in my thirty-five years of service, I certainly had a few frightening
5 experiences.

When I was young, I took a job in a newly built lighthouse off the coast of Guiana. The lighthouse was very isolated. It was about twenty miles from land. The pay was high, though, and I wanted to save money before I married.

10 The lighthouse stood on a small rock named Three Skeleton Key. It had earned its name from the story of three men who had escaped from prison in a stolen canoe. Their canoe wrecked on the rock, and the men eventually died of hunger and thirst. When the men were discovered, nothing
15 remained but three heaps of bones. The story was that the three skeletons danced over the small rock, screaming. . . .

Three Skeleton Key was an island of black rock. It was about one hundred fifty feet long, perhaps forty feet wide. The rocks were dangerously smooth. One wrong step, and
20 you'd fall into the sea. The sea was full of sharks.

Still, it was a nice life there. During the day, we would clean the rooms and the light itself. At night, we would sit on the balcony and watch the strong white bar of light shine over the sea. My fellow keepers were named Le Gleo and
25 Itchoua. We liked our life on the key.

"Three Skeleton Key" by George G. Toudouze adapted from *Esquire,* January 1937.
Copyright 1937 by Hearst Communications, Inc. All rights reserved. Esquire is a
trademark of Hearst Magazines Property, Inc. Retold by Holt, Rinehart and Winston.
Reproduced by permission of **Esquire Magazine.**

One night, Itchoua called Le Gleo and me from our rooms. We climbed to the balcony and stood beside him.

Itchoua pointed out to the sea. There we saw a big ship heading straight toward us. It was an odd course, we thought. 30 Ships were a rare sight in our waters. Our lighthouse existed to warn ships away from the rocks, so most ships steered clear of us.

Le Gleo cried out, "What's wrong with the ship's crew? Are they all drunk or insane? Can't they see us?"

35 Itchoua looked at us sharply and said, "See us? I'm sure they do—if there *is* a crew aboard!"

Then we understood the ship's odd behavior. For some reason, the ship's crew had abandoned it. Then, the ship had sailed by itself, guided by the wind.

40 We kept watching as the ship sailed on. In the light of our lantern, the ship seemed strong. Itchoua cried out, "Why was the ship abandoned? Nothing is smashed. There's no sign of fire. And, it doesn't look like it's sinking."

For the next four hours, the ship played around us. It 45 zigzagged, stopped, and then suddenly sailed forward.

When dawn broke, we got out our binoculars to inspect the ship.

Just then, the wind rose, and the ship changed course. It headed straight for us again. This time, it came very close. 50 We knew it could not turn in time.

All this time, we kept our binoculars aimed at the ship. We suddenly cried out together, "The rats!"

Now we knew why the ship was sailing without a crew. The crew had been driven out by rats. The rats of the sea are 55 large, strong, intelligent, and brave. If you harm one, his sharp cry will bring crowds of his fellows to tear your flesh. They will not stop until nothing is left of you but bones.

Here's HOW

MAKING PREDICTIONS

Why is the ship sailing so close to the lighthouse? I bet the crew has a message for the men in the lighthouse. Or maybe the crew is in trouble?

Your TURN

SUSPENSE AND FORESHADOWING

Re-read lines 28–50. Why doesn't the writer tell us right away what has happened to the ship? How does that passage make you feel?

_____

_____

_____

_____

_____

_____

At times, the rats will attack a ship's crew. They either drive them from the ship or eat them alive. Studying the ship,
60 I turned sick. Its lifeboats were all in place. Its crew had not abandoned ship.

The ship came for us at full speed. It crashed on a sharp point of rock and then split in two. It sank like a stone.

But the rats did not drown. They sprang along the masts
65 and onto the rocks right before the ship sank. Then they noticed us—fresh meat.

We barely had time to jump back. We closed the door leading to the balcony, and we went down the stairs. We shut every window tightly. It didn't take long for the horrible
70 group of rats to run up the tower. They scratched at the glass. There were so many rats that it seemed as if a fur coat covered the tower. Just a few millimeters of glass separated our faces from their beady eyes, sharp claws, and teeth. We were sealed alive in our own lighthouse. We were prisoners
75 of a horde of starving rats.

When night came, we lit the light. As the light turned, it blinded thousands of rats crowded against the glass. Their cries were so loud we had to shout to hear one another. We couldn't sleep all night.

80 The next day, we were calmer. We had fun by teasing the rats. We would place our faces against the glass. The rats couldn't understand the invisible barrier that separated us from them. But, the day after that, we realized how serious our position was. The air in the lighthouse smelled of rats. Of
85 course, we couldn't open the windows to get fresh air.

The morning of the fourth day, I saw that the wooden frame of my window had been eaten away from the outside. I called Le Gleo and Itchoua. They helped me seal the window over with a sheet of tin. When we finished, Itchoua pointed

90 at the tin plate. "If that gives way," he said, "they can change the name of the place to Six Skeleton Key."

The next six days and seven nights, we had nothing to do but watch clusters of rats fall from the rock. The rats would fall a hundred and twenty feet into the water. There the
95 sharks could eat them. It didn't seem to matter, though. There were still so many rats left.

We thought often of those three prisoners who had died on the rock. We imagined our bones joining theirs. The darkness of our prison increased our gloom. We had to seal
100 every window with tin. The only light came in through the lantern room at the very top of the tower.

Le Gleo had nightmares where he saw the three skeletons of the prisoners dancing around him. His crazy descriptions were so clear that Itchoua and I began to see the three
105 skeletons, too.

There was only one thing left to do. We decided not to light the lantern on the ninth night. This is never done unless the lighthouse keepers are dead. The light is necessary to warn ships away from the rock. But that night, Three
110 Skeleton Key was dark.

At two in the morning, the sheet of metal sealing Itchoua's window gave way. Itchoua just had time to leap to his feet and cry for help. The three of us fought the maddened rats that flowed through the open window.

115 They bit. We struck them down with our knives. Then, we went back up the stairs, fighting off the rats that leaped on us. We found ourselves on the floor of the lantern room. We had no food or drink. We were bleeding all over. Our clothes were shredded.

120 Le Gleo stared at Itchoua and me. Then he looked at the rats and began laughing horribly, "Hee! Hee! The Three Skeletons! Hee! Hee! The Three Skeletons are now *six* skeletons! *Six* skeletons!"

SUSPENSE AND FORESHADOWING

Why does Itchoua say that the name of the island can be changed to Six Skeleton Key (lines 89–91)?

_____

_____

_____

_____

_____

Your
TURN

MAKING PREDICTIONS

The men in the lighthouse are being attacked by rats. They are cut off from their supplies (line 118). Do you think they'll survive? Explain your prediction.

_____

_____

_____

_____

_____

_____

SUSPENSE AND FORESHADOWING

As you read about the rescue crew's arrival, what questions are on your mind? Write your questions below.

_____

_____

_____

_____

_____

SUSPENSE AND FORESHADOWING

Do you enjoy scary stories? Why or why not?

_____

_____

_____

_____

_____

_____

He threw his head back and laughed. I did the only thing
125 I could—I swung the back of my hand across his face. His laughing stopped. Then, he began to cry like a child.

As morning arrived, the patrol came to find out why our lighthouse was dark. Through my binoculars, I could see the horrified faces of the patrol officers and crew. I learned later
130 that they thought we had been eaten alive.

The crew were about to leave when Itchoua managed to signal them. They signaled back.

The patrol boat came back at noon, along with a supply ship, two small coast-guard boats, and a fireboat.

135 The fireboat's powerful jet of water knocked many rats from the tower into the sea. There the sharks gulped them down. Yet more rats swam out to the fireboat. The men were forced to fight the rats with their bare hands. At last, all but one of the boats left. All that night, Le Gleo raved about
140 skeletons, while Itchoua and I burned with fever.

The next afternoon, I saw a tugboat towing a huge barge filled with meat. The tugboat dragged the barge close to the island. The rats swam out and boarded it. The tug dragged the barge about a mile from shore. There, the barge was
145 soaked in gasoline and set on fire.

As the barge burned, the rats tried to escape. A patrol boat bombed them. The sharks finished off the rest.

A small boat from the patrol boat took us off to the hospital. Le Gleo's mind had cracked; he went completely
150 crazy. He was locked up in an insane asylum, the poor man! Itchoua's bites were infected; he died within a week.

As for me—when they aired out the lighthouse and repaired the damage done by the rats, I returned to Three Skeleton Key. Why not? I liked the place. To be honest, it was
155 the most pleasant job I ever had.

Suspense and Foreshadowing

"Uh-oh. What's under the bed?" "Is he going to look under the bed?"
A good **suspense** writer has you wondering what's going to happen next. To
heighten the suspense, a writer will use clues, or **foreshadowing,** to
suggest events that will happen later in the story. These clues lead you to
ask many questions.

What kinds of questions did you ask yourself when you were reading
"Three Skeleton Key"? Chart your reading below. In the first column, read
the foreshadowing clues. In the second column, write the questions that
were in your mind when you read each clue in the story. In the third
column, write what happens in the story to answer your question. Part
of the chart has been filled in for you.

Foreshadowing Clues	My Questions	What Happens in the Story
1. The narrator tells the story of how Three Skeleton Key got its name. (lines 10–16)		
2. The men try to guess why the ship is sailing so close to the lighthouse. (lines 28–52)		
3. The wooden frame of the window is eaten away by the rats. (lines 86–87)	Oh, no. What will the men do? Will the rats get into the lighthouse?	The men put up a sheet of tin to seal the window, but the rats get in anyway.
4. The fireboat tries to knock the rats off the tower with a powerful jet of water. The plan doesn't work, so the rescue team leaves. (lines 135–139)		

Eeking Out a Life

Reading Skill: Structure and Purpose of a Newspaper Article

The **purpose** of a newspaper article is to give you information about current events. A good article gives you the facts. It answers the questions *who? what? when? where? why?* and *how?*

The **structure** of many newspaper articles is like an upside-down pyramid. The most important information is at the top. The least important information is at the bottom.

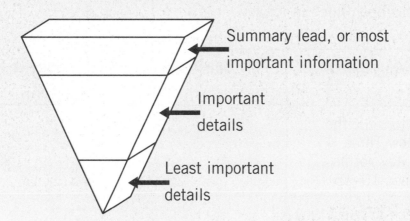

Summary lead, or most important information

Important details

Least important details

Into the Article

This newspaper article is the story of a lost rat. Many people think rats are dirty, dangerous animals. But some rats are very clean and make good pets. This little rat may have had an owner who lost him. Nobody knows. But he certainly found a good home, even though he must share it with two dogs and three cats.

Based on the Newspaper Article by
Matt Surman

Eeking Out a Life

Here's
HOW

VOCABULARY

"Eeking Out a Life." I'm not sure I know what *eek* means. I think it's a word to show fright, but that doesn't make sense. I'll look in the dictionary. Here's *eke out*. It means "to get with difficulty." Maybe the rat has a hard life. Aha! The word *eke* is pronounced like *eek*. I think the author is playing with words.

Here's
HOW

STRUCTURE AND PURPOSE

In lines 1–6, I see that the *who* in the story is a rat named Sunny Jim and two humans. The *what* is the fact that they rescued him.

Your
TURN

STRUCTURE AND PURPOSE

Read the rest of the article to answer the questions *where, how,* and *why.* Write your answers on the lines below.

_____

_____

_____

1   **S**unny Jim was once a rat alone in the wilderness. Who knows what dangers he faced?

Was he chased by hungry owls? Did sewer rats go after him? Did he search for a child who lost him?

5   His new owners can only guess. Hayley Huttenmaier and her fiancé Nachshon Rose rescued the little rat.

Rose was out walking when he found him. The rat ran past him and hid. Gradually he emerged and sat on Rose's shoe.

10   Clearly the white and brownish-gray rat was a pet. He was clean and friendly and tiny. So Rose carried him home. Huttenmaier and Rose already had two dogs and three cats.

Now Sunny Jim lives inside a cabinet. He has a little
15   room with brick walls. He has toys, a soft bed, and plenty of food.

Huttenmaier believes a child lost the rat. They placed an ad, but no one has called. Rose doesn't want to give Sunny back. He believes the rat was unwanted by its
20   owner, or that parents made their child abandon the little rat.

Is owning him dangerous? Experts agree he's not a danger.

According to Louis Stack, pet rats are like little dogs.
25   "You can watch TV with them sitting on your shoulder."

Stack belongs to the American Fancy Rat and Mouse Association. Its members raise and show rats the way people show dogs.

Sunny's owners are happy to give him a safe home.
30   Maybe they'll get him a friend some day. Then there'll be a Rat Pack.

"Eeking Out a Life" by Matt Surman adapted from *The Los Angeles Times,* July 8, 2000. Copyright © 2000 by **The Los Angeles Times.** Retold by Holt, Rinehart and Winston. Reproduced by permission of the publisher.

Inverted Pyramid Structure

Many newspaper articles have a structure that is like an upside-down pyramid. First, the most important information is given. Then, important details are given. They are followed by less important details.

After you read "Eeking Out a Life," fill in the upside-down pyramid below with details from the story. Some "Least Important Details" have been put in the pyramid for you.

Summary Lead, or Most Important Information

Important Details

Least Important Details

Pet rats are like little dogs.
You can watch TV with
them sitting on your
shoulder.

Cellular Telephone Owner's Manual

Reading Skill: Sequence

When you are reading an owner's manual, it is often important to follow steps in **sequence.** You must complete one step before you begin the next step. Otherwise, you may damage your expensive machine. You may find it helpful to make a chart and list all the steps in sequence.

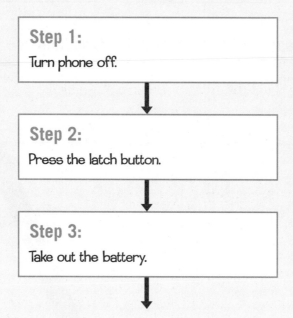

Step 1:
Turn phone off.

Step 2:
Press the latch button.

Step 3:
Take out the battery.

Into the Manual

Many things around your house today need batteries to work. You may have a portable phone in the bedroom, a small CD player in the kitchen, or a remote control in the living room. These items may use different types of batteries. They also probably use different methods for installing the batteries. When changing batteries you will need to follow the instructions in the owner's manual carefully.

Changing the Battery

There are two ways to remove and replace your battery.

Standard Method

1. Turn off your telephone.
2. Press the latch button on the back of the battery. Then, slide the battery down until it stops.
3. Carefully take out the battery.
4. To replace the battery, line up a new battery on the grooves. Slide it upward in the direction of the arrows until it clicks into place.

Quick-Change Method

This method lets you replace the battery during a phone call.

1. Tell the person you're talking to that you are going to change the battery.
2. Remove the battery from the cell phone.
3. Put in the extra battery. (Be sure it has been charged up and is ready to use.)
4. Press PWR (power). This will return you to your telephone call. You have five seconds to press PWR before your call is disconnected.

The quick-change method allows you to replace the battery during a telephone call. This is useful if you see the "low battery" message during a call.

It is a good idea to practice this method before trying it during a real phone call.

Here's
HOW

SEQUENCE

In step 2 of the Standard Method, I see that I need to press the latch button before I take the battery out. If I tried to take the battery out before I pressed the latch button, I might break something in the phone.

Your
TURN

SEQUENCE

One sentence in steps 1–4 of the Quick-Change Method makes it clear why you should read these instructions carefully. Circle the sentence that tells you what will happen if you don't press PWR in time.

Sequence Charts

Below are two sequence charts for changing a cellular telephone battery. There is one chart for the Standard Method and one for the Quick-Change Method. Fill in the boxes for the steps that have been left out.

Standard Method:

> **Step 1:**

↓

> **Step 2:**
> Press the latch button.

↓

> **Step 3:**
> Take out the battery.

↓

> **Step 4:**

Quick-Change Method:

> **Step 1:**
> Warn the person you are talking to.

↓

> **Step 2:**

↓

> **Step 3:**

↓

> **Step 4:**

Sequence Charts

On the previous page, you filled in two sequence charts. These charts described the process for changing the battery in a cellular telephone. Now, make a sequence chart that shows the process for something you know how to do. You might describe the process of how to wash dishes or how to bathe the dog. You could describe how to do an Internet search for baseball statistics. You might describe how to get from your house to a place you know well. You might even describe how to set up a tent. If you need more boxes for your sequence chart, add as many as you need.

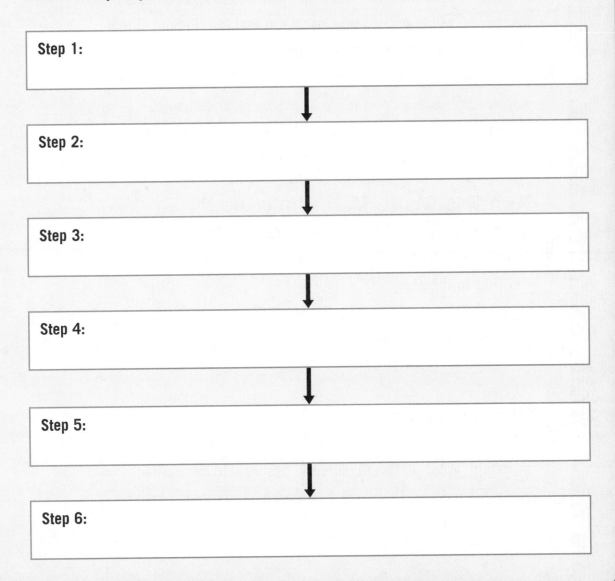

Step 1:

Step 2:

Step 3:

Step 4:

Step 5:

Step 6:

Mother and Daughter

Literary Focus: Character

A **character** is anyone who plays a part in a story. A **character trait** is a quality that a person carries on the inside. For instance, when you say a person is generous, or insecure, you are talking about character traits. (By contrast, if you say someone has brown hair or blue eyes, you are talking about physical traits, or appearance.)

Most writers want you to get to know fictional characters just as you would get to know people in real life. People in real life don't wear T-shirts that say "SNOBBY and CONCEITED" or "FRIENDLY WITH A GOOD SENSE OF HUMOR." In the same way, writers usually don't tell you directly what a character is like. Instead, they want you to read very closely and get to know the characters and their traits yourself.

Reading Skill: Making Inferences

To decide what a character is like, you usually have to make inferences. **Inferences** are educated guesses based on clues you find in the story.

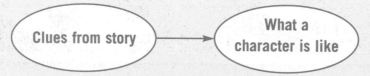

Into the Story

Parents and children don't always agree on what's most important. What do you think is the best way to deal with these differences? Think about which character traits make it easier for people to work out their problems with each other.

Mother and Daughter

BASED ON THE STORY BY
Gary Soto

Here's HOW

CHARACTER

What kind of person waves to people she doesn't even know? Mrs. Moreno is outgoing and friendly. She doesn't care that people stare at her because she's so large. She just wears what's comfortable.

Here's HOW

MAKING INFERENCES

What Mrs. Moreno does in lines 13–19 is funny, but I think she's more interested in playing a joke than in her daughter's feelings.

Here's HOW

MAKING INFERENCES

Yollie could have responded in many ways to her mother's joke. For example, she could have called her mother names, or she could have cried herself to sleep. Instead, Yollie decides to play a joke on her mother. I think this means the two have an easygoing, fun-loving relationship.

---

1   Yollie's mother, Mrs. Moreno, was a large woman. She wore a muumuu[1] and butterfly-shaped glasses. She liked to water her lawn in the evening and wave at cars passing by. Now and then a driver would shout *"Mamacita!"*[2] But most

5   of the time they just stared and wondered how she got so large.

   Mrs. Moreno had a strange sense of humor. Once, Yollie and her mother were watching a late-night horror movie. But Yollie couldn't keep her eyes open. "Mom, wake me up when

10   the movie's over so I can go to bed," mumbled Yollie.

   "OK, Yollie, I wake you," said her mother through a mouthful of popcorn.

   But after the movie ended, Mrs. Moreno didn't wake Yollie up. Instead, she laughed under her breath, turned the TV and

15   lights off, and tiptoed to bed. Yollie woke up in the middle of the night and didn't know where she was. For a moment, she thought she was dead. She looked around in the darkness and called, "Mom? Mom, where are you?" But there was no answer.

20   Finally, Yollie realized that her mother had gone to bed. It was another of her little jokes. But Yollie wasn't laughing. She tiptoed into her mother's bedroom with a glass of water and set it on the nightstand next to the bed. When her mother got up, she overturned the glass and screamed.

25   "Ha! Ha! I got you back," Yollie laughed.

   Despite their jokes, mother and daughter usually got along. They watched bargain matinees[3] together, and played

---

1. **muumuu** (MOO moo): a loose-fitting, bright-colored, Hawaiian dress, usually worn casually.
2. *Mamacita* (ma ma SEE tah): Spanish for "little mama."
3. **matinees** (MAT n AYZ): afternoon performances of a play or movie.

"Mother and Daughter" adapted from *Baseball and Other Stories* by Gary Soto. Copyright © 1990 by Gary Soto. Retold by Holt, Rinehart and Winston. Reproduced by permission of **Harcourt, Inc.**

croquet[4] in the summer and checkers in the winter.
Mrs. Moreno encouraged Yollie to study hard. She wanted
30 her daughter to be a doctor.

"*Tienes que estudiar mucho,*" Mrs. Moreno would say.
"You have to study a lot, then you can get a good job and
take care of me."

"Yes, Mama," Yollie would respond, her face buried in a
35 book. If she gave her mother any sympathy, Mrs. Moreno
would begin her stories. She would tell how she had come
from Mexico with nothing on her back but a sack.

Everyone thought Yollie's mother was funny. Her brother
Raul, a nightclub owner, thought she was funny enough to go
40 into show business.

But there was nothing funny about Yollie needing a new
outfit for the eighth-grade fall dance. They couldn't afford[5]
one. The little money Mrs. Moreno had saved was for Yollie's
college education.

45 The best Mrs. Moreno could do was buy Yollie a pair of
black shoes with velvet bows and fabric dye to color her
white summer dress black.

"We can color your dress so it will look brand-new," her
mother said. She poured the black liquid into a tub.

50 Yollie didn't want to watch. She *knew* it wouldn't work. It
would be like the time her mother stirred up a batch of
molasses for candy apples on Yollie's birthday. The apples
turned out as hard as rocks and hurt the kids' teeth. Finally,
they had a contest to see who could break the apples open by
55 throwing them against the wall. Everyone went home happy.

To Yollie's surprise, the dress came out shiny black. It
looked brand-new. She smiled at her mother, who hugged
Yollie and said, "See, what did I tell you?"

---

4. croquet (croh KAY): a game in which players use mallets, which look like big
hammers, to hit wooden balls through wire hoops on the lawn.
5. afford (uh FAWRD): pay for.

VOCABULARY

Help! What is Mrs. Moreno saying in line 31? I know *mucho* means "a lot" in Spanish, but otherwise I have no clue. Oh, I get it. The writer repeats the phrase in English right there in line 32. The Spanish sentence probably means something like "You have to study a lot."

MAKING INFERENCES

Re-read lines 51–56. Was Yollie's birthday party a success? Why, or why not? What's another way the party could have turned out?

_____

_____

_____

_____

_____

_____

Here's HOW

MAKING INFERENCES

At first, Yollie is worried about her mother's plan, but when the plan works, she smiles (line 57). Yollie might get frustrated with her mother sometimes, but she doesn't hold on to bad feelings.

Your TURN

CHARACTER

Re-read lines 81–83. What does Yollie's action tell you about her character?

60 The dance was important to Yollie because she was in love with Ernie Castillo, the third-best speller in the class. She bathed, dressed, and did her hair and nails. Then she jumped into the car.

Mrs. Moreno let Yollie out in front of the school. She waved and told her to have a good time.

65 Yollie ran into her best friend, Janice. They didn't say it, but each thought the other was the most beautiful girl at the dance. All the boys would want to dance with them.

The evening was warm but thick with clouds. Paper lanterns in the trees made the evening seem romantic. 70 Everyone danced, sipped punch, and stood in groups of threes and fours, talking.

Yollie kept smoothing her dress down when the wind picked it up. She had her eye on Ernie. It turned out that Ernie had his eye on Yollie, too. He ate a handful of cookies 75 nervously and then asked her for a dance.

"Sure," she said. She almost threw herself into his arms.

As they danced, rain began falling. Yollie loved the sound of the raindrops ticking against the leaves. She leaned her head on Ernie's shoulder. He felt warm and tender.[6] Yollie 80 could tell he was in love with her.

It began to pour. The girls hurried to the restrooms. One girl cried because her velvet dress was wet. Yollie felt sorry for her and helped her dry the dress off with paper towels.

Yollie went to a mirror. Her mother's makeup had washed 85 away. She combed her damp hair. She couldn't wait to get back to Ernie.

Yollie looked down, and shame spread across her face. A black puddle was forming at her feet. The dye was falling from her dress like black tears. Yollie saw that her dress was

---

6. tender: gentle, kind.

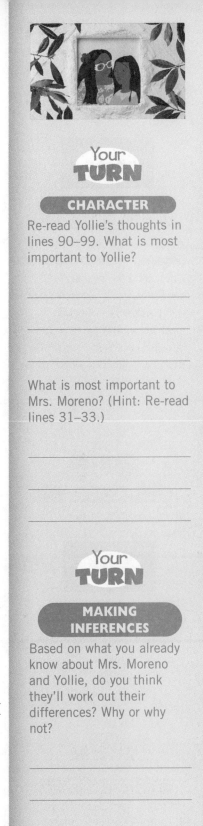

90 gray. She looked around. Everyone would laugh. They would know that she dyed an old dress because she couldn't afford a new one. She hurried from the restroom with her head down. She raced home, crying as the rain mixed with her tears.

95 When she arrived home, her mother was on the couch eating cookies and watching TV.

"How was the dance, *m'ija?*"[7]

Yollie ran to her bedroom. She undressed and threw the dress on the floor.

100 Her mother came into the room, "What's wrong, baby?"

"The dress. It's cheap! It's no good!" Yollie kicked the dress at her mother and watched it land in her hands. Mrs. Moreno studied it closely but couldn't see what was wrong. "What's the matter? It's just a bit wet."

105 "The dye came out, that's what."

Mrs. Moreno looked at her hands and saw the grayish dye. Poor baby, she thought. She wanted to tell her daughter how sorry she was. But she knew it wouldn't help. She walked back to the living room and cried.

110 The next morning, mother and daughter stayed away from each other. Yollie sat in her room. Her mother watered her plants with a Pepsi bottle.

"Drink, my children," she said loudly enough for Yollie to hear. "Water is all you need. My daughter needs clothes, but I 115 don't have any money."

Yollie was embarrassed about what she had said to her mother last night. It wasn't her mother's fault that they were poor.

---

7. *m'ija* (MEE ha): Spanish for "my daughter."

Your TURN

CHARACTER

Re-read Yollie's thoughts in lines 90–99. What is most important to Yollie?

_____

_____

_____

What is most important to Mrs. Moreno? (Hint: Re-read lines 31–33.)

_____

_____

_____

Your TURN

MAKING INFERENCES

Based on what you already know about Mrs. Moreno and Yollie, do you think they'll work out their differences? Why or why not?

_____

_____

_____

_____

_____

Your
TURN

CHARACTER

How does Mrs. Moreno change by the end of the story? Do you find this change believable? Explain.

_____

_____

_____

_____

_____

_____

When they sat down together for lunch, they both felt
120 awkward.[8] But Mrs. Moreno had made a fresh stack of
tortillas[9] and cooked up a pan of *chile verde*. That broke the
ice. She licked her thumb and smacked her lips.

"You know, honey, we have to figure a way to make
money," Yollie's mother said. "You and me. We don't have to
125 be poor. Maybe we could invent something."

"What can we make?" asked Yollie. She took another
tortilla.

The mother looked around for ideas, but then shrugged.
"Let's forget it. It's better to get an education. If you have
130 spare time then maybe you can invent something."

The phone rang. Yollie leaned over from her chair to
answer it. It was Ernie wondering why she had left. He was
glad to find out that she wasn't mad at him. He asked if she
would like to go to a movie.

135 "I'll ask," Yollie said, smiling. She covered the phone with
her hand and counted to ten. Then she said, "My mom says
it's OK. What are we going to see?"

After Yollie hung up, her mother climbed onto a chair to
reach the top shelf in the hall closet. She reached behind a
140 stack of towels and pushed her chubby hand into a cigar box.
There she kept a secret stash of money.

"I've been saving a little money every month," said Mrs.
Moreno. "For you, *m'ija*." Her mother held up five twenties.
The green money smelled sweeter than flowers. They drove
145 to Macy's and bought a blouse, shoes, and a skirt that would
not bleed in rain or any other weather.

---

8. **awkward** (AWK wuhrd): embarrassed; uncomfortable.
9. **tortillas** (tawr TEE uhz): round, thin pieces of bread made from cornmeal or wheat flour. *Tortilla* means "little cake" in Spanish.

Character

Most writers don't like to *tell* you directly what a character is like.
Instead, they like to *show* you through details in the story. For instance, a
writer might not tell you directly that a character is nervous. Instead, you
can reach your own conclusion by looking at details in the story, such as
these: "She was biting her nails"; "Her suit was a sweat-soaked, wrinkled
mess"; "Her eyes shifted around the room."

Cluster Diagram

Choose three words that describe Mrs. Moreno in "Mother and Daughter."
Write those words under her name below. Then, draw a circle around each
word. Now, go back to the story and find examples of how the writer
shows you those character traits. Jot down the examples, circle them, and
draw lines connecting them to the main circle. The diagram has already
been started for you.

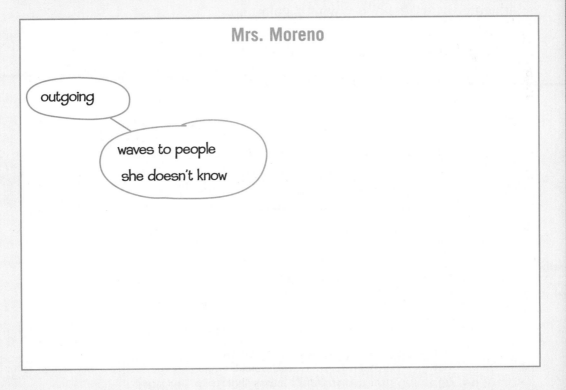

The Smallest Dragonboy

Literary Focus: Motivation

Your little brother gives you his favorite book. You might wonder, "Why did he do that?" Or say a classmate never says hello to you. You might ask yourself, "What makes her act that way?" These are questions about motivation. **Motivation** is the reason for someone's behavior.

Sometimes a writer tells you the characters' motivation directly. Other times you must figure out for yourself why the characters act as they do.

Reading Skill: Making Inferences

Reading a story is a little like being a detective. Writers do not always tell you directly what's happening. Sometimes you need to find clues in the story and then make **inferences** (educated guesses) about what's going on.

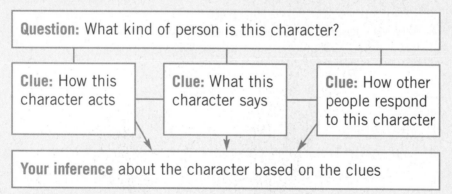

Question: What kind of person is this character?

Clue: How this character acts

Clue: What this character says

Clue: How other people respond to this character

Your inference about the character based on the clues

Into the Story

The author's brother Kevin was the inspiration for this story. As a child, Kevin suffered from a painful bone disease. He seemed to be marked as an underdog—a loser. However, his courage let him triumph over difficulties. Do you know someone who was an underdog but ended up a winner?

The Smallest Dragonboy

BASED ON THE STORY BY
Anne McCaffrey

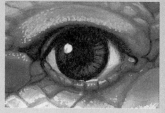

Here's
HOW

VOCABULARY

So, this story takes place on an imaginary planet. It sounds like science fiction to me. I know that science fiction writers sometimes make up new words to make their imaginary places seem more real. I'll pay attention to made-up vocabulary as I read.

Your
TURN

VOCABULARY

Look up the word *impress* in a dictionary, and write its meaning below. Notice that in this story, the word is capitalized. As you read, think about what *Impress* means in this story.

_____

_____

_____

_____

_____

_____

_____

_____

YOU NEED TO KNOW   You are about to enter the imaginary world of Pern, located somewhere in outer space. Pern is threatened by the dangerous Red Star. This star rains deadly threadlike plant spores (reproductive bodies) on Pern every two hundred years or so. If Thread falls on Pern soil and grows there, it will destroy every living being.

The people on Pern want to protect their planet. So, they have created a race of great winged dragons. When fed a special black rock called firestone, the dragons can breathe flames that burn Thread to ashes. During Threadfall, the dragons and their dragonriders charge into battle in midair. They live inside the cones of volcanoes. These cave colonies are called Weyrs.

As the story opens, young candidates for dragonrider in Benden Weyr wait for some dragon eggs to hatch. Each newborn dragon will choose its own rider—a lifelong partner. This process of choosing a partner is called Impression.

1   **K**eevan couldn't keep up with the other candidates. Beterli was the oldest boy, and he led the group. Keevan was sure that Beterli had set a fast pace just to embarrass him. Keevan would arrive at the end of the group. He'd be out of breath, and the instructor would be angry.

5   Dragonriders had to be on time. This was true even for candidates. The Weyrleader[1] of Benden Weyr did not put up with laziness. A good record was especially important now. It

---

1. Weyrleader (WEHR lee duhr): the male leader of a Weyr, a cave colony on the planet Pern. Benden Weyr is the name of a specific weyr.

Adaptation of "The Smallest Dragonboy" by Anne McCaffrey. Copyright © 1973, 2001 by Anne McCaffrey. First appeared in *Science Fiction Tales*. Retold by Holt, Rinehart and Winston. Reproduced by permission of **Anne McCaffrey and agent, Virginia Kidd.**

was near hatching time. The candidates were waiting hopefully for the glowing eggs. The eggs were hardening on
10 the hot sands of the Hatching Ground cave. Baby dragons would crack their spotted shells and stagger[2] out to choose their lifetime companions.

Just the thought of that great moment made Keevan's breath catch in his throat. To be chosen—to be a dragonrider!
15 He could sit on his winged dragon. The dragon would be his friend for life. They would use a special type of communication—telepathy—so that they could read each other's thoughts. They would understand each other without having to speak to each other. The dragon would be Keevan's
20 friend in good times and in fighting times. They would fly without effort over the lands of Pern!

But Keevan worried that he'd never become a dragonrider because he was too small. People were always calling him "babe." Keevan had to work twice as hard as any other boy
25 his age to prove himself.

Besides, no one knew exactly what Impressed the baby dragons as they struggled from their shells in search of lifetime partners.

"I like to believe that dragons see into a man's heart,"
30 Keevan's foster mother, Mende, told him. "If they find goodness, honesty, a flexible mind, patience, courage—and you've got all that, dear Keevan—that's what dragons look for. I've seen many a well-grown boy left standing on the sands, on Hatching Day, in favor of someone not so strong or
35 tall or handsome. I don't believe that F'lar, our Weyrleader, was all that tall when the bronze dragon chose him."

Keevan certainly never dreamed of Impressing a bronze. Maybe he had a chance to Impress a green dragon. Green

2. **stagger** (STAG uhr): to move from side to side as if about to fall.

THE SMALLEST DRAGONBOY   **41**

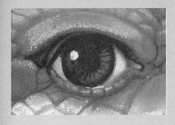

Here's HOW

VOCABULARY

What does *telepathy* mean? Oh, I see, the writer explains what it means right here in lines 16–19.

Your TURN

MOTIVATION

In lines 13–25, the writer takes you into Keevan's mind. You learn what drives, or *motivates*, him. Circle the paragraph that explains why Keevan works so hard. Then, answer these questions:

1. What does Keevan want?

_____

_____

_____

_____

2. What does Keevan fear?

_____

_____

_____

_____

_____

Here's HOW

MOTIVATION

Wow! I see from lines 47–51 why these boys are so competitive. I think the Impression is the most important event in Pern society. It affects the boys' lives forever. No wonder the boys are nervous. I'm still wondering, though, why Beterli is so mean. The writer doesn't tell us Beterli's motivation directly.

Your TURN

MAKING INFERENCES

Since the writer doesn't state Beterli's motivation directly, you'll have to make an inference from the clues in the text. Re-read lines 64–65. What do you think Beterli is afraid of?

_____

_____

_____

_____

_____

_____

dragons were small and fast, and there were more of them.
40 But to fly a bronze? A bronze rider could hope to become a Weyrleader!

They arrived at the Hatching Ground. "Impression time is close, candidates," the instructor was saying. All the candidates were surrounding him. "See the stretch marks on
45 this promising egg." The stretch marks *were* larger than yesterday.

"I'd say the great opening day is nearly here," the instructor went on. Then his face became serious. "As we well know, there are only forty eggs and seventy-two
50 candidates. Some of you may be disappointed on the great day."

Some of the boys laughed nervously. Everyone started to walk among the eggs. Beterli stepped up to "his" egg, daring anyone to come near it. Keevan smiled, because he had
55 already touched it without Beterli seeing.

"I don't know why you're allowed in this Impression, Keevan. There are enough of us without a babe," Beterli said, shaking his head.

"I'm of age." Keevan kept his voice calm. He told himself
60 not to be bothered by Beterli's words.

Beterli stood on his toe tips. "You can't even see over an egg. Hatching Day, you'd better get in front, or the dragons won't see you at all."

"You'd better make sure a dragon sees *you* this time,
65 Beterli," Keevan replied. "You're almost too old, aren't you?"

Beterli's face went red. He took a step forward, his hand half raised. Keevan stood his ground, but if Beterli came any closer, he would call the instructor. No one fought on the Hatching Ground. Surely Beterli knew that.
70 Fortunately, at that moment, the instructor called the boys together. He led them from the Hatching Ground to start on

evening chores. Firestone sacks had to be filled against Thread attack, and black rock brought to the kitchen hearths.

After the chores were done, people of the Weyr began to
75 gather for the evening meal. The dragonriders came in from the Feeding Ground. Tonight Keevan's father, K'last, was at the main dragonrider table.

K'last and another dragonrider, L'vel, were discussing the age of the candidates. L'vel thought that only the older boys
80 should be candidates. But K'last insisted that any boy over twelve had the right to stand in the Hatching Ground.

"Only a dragon knows what he wants in a rider. We certainly can't tell. Time and again people are surprised by the dragons' choices," K'last smiled and looked around the
85 table. "The dragons never seem to make mistakes, though."

"Now, K'last, just look at the list of boys for this Impression. Seventy-two boys and only forty eggs. Drop off the twelve youngest, and there's still plenty for the hatchlings to choose from."

90 "Half the Weyr-bred[3] lads have already been through several Impressions," one of the bronze riders said. "Let's drop some of *them* this time. Give the new ones a chance."

Everyone argued all through dinner. When the evening meal was over, no decision had been made. The Weyrleader
95 promised to consider the matter, though.

Not many candidates slept that night. The boys were feeling unsure of themselves as they were called out of bed for morning chores. Keevan's foster mother, Mende, had to tell Keevan twice that he was being clumsy.

100 "What is the matter with you, boy?" she asked when he missed the bin and dropped black rock all over the ground.

"They're going to keep me from this Impression."

"What?" Mende stared at him. "Who?"

---

3. **Weyr-bred:** raised in a Weyr.

Here's HOW

VOCABULARY

What are *hearths* (line 73)? Let me see what I can get from the story. Well, I know the hearths are in the kitchen. I also know that the boys are bringing black rock to the hearths. In the You Need to Know section to this story, I read that dragons eat this black rock to breathe flames that burn Thread. So, hearths are something hot and in the kitchen. Oh, I get it—ovens! My dictionary says that a *hearth* is a fireplace or brick oven. So, I was right!

Your TURN

MOTIVATION

Re-read lines 96–99. Why is Keevan being so clumsy? What was going through his mind when the men were talking at dinner?

"You heard them talking at dinner last night. The babes
105 won't be allowed at the hatching."

Mende looked at him a moment longer. Then, she touched his arm gently. "There's lots of talk around a supper table, Keevan. And it ends with supper. I've heard the same nonsense before every hatching. Nothing is ever changed,
110 though."

"There's always a first time," Keevan answered.

"That'll be enough of that, Keevan. Finish your job. All my fosterlings[4] make dragonriders."

"The first time?" Keevan was bold enough to ask as he
115 went off to get rock.

If Beterli hadn't been getting rock at the same time, things might have turned out differently, Keevan thought later. Keevan was gathering a second load of rock when Beterli arrived.

120 "Have you heard the news, babe?" Beterli asked. He was grinning from ear to ear.

"The eggs are cracking?" Keevan nearly dropped the loaded shovel.

"No! Guess again!" Beterli was much too pleased with
125 himself.

"I don't have time for guessing games," Keevan said, pretending not to care. He began to shovel black rock as fast as he could.

Beterli grabbed the shovel from Keevan's hands. "Guess!"
130 he said.

"Give me my shovel, Beterli!" Keevan stood up tall, but he still didn't come to Beterli's shoulders. Other boys suddenly appeared around them.

---

4. **fosterlings** (FAWS tuhr lihngz): foster children; used in Old English.

He grabbed the shovel from Beterli. The older boy tried to
135 get it back. But Keevan held the handle tightly.

With a sudden movement, Beterli rammed the handle into
Keevan's chest. He knocked Keevan over. Keevan felt a sharp
pain behind his left ear, a terrible pain in his left shin, and
then he felt nothing.

140 The next morning, Mende's voice woke him. Keevan
though he had slept in, so he tried to throw back the covers.
But he couldn't move. He was tucked firmly into his bed.
And then the tight bandage on his head and the ache in his
leg brought back recent events.

145 "Hatching?" he cried.

"No, lovey," Mende said in a kind voice. Her hand was
cool and gentle on his forehead. "Though some people won't
be at any hatching ever again." Her voice was stern.

Keevan looked behind Mende and saw the Weyrwoman,[5]
150 Lessa. She had a frown on her face.

"Keevan, will you tell me what happened?" asked Lessa in
an even voice.

He remembered Beterli now and the fight over the shovel.
. . . What had Mende said about some not being at any
155 hatching? Much as he hated Beterli, he couldn't bring himself
to tattle on Beterli and force him out of the Impression.

The Weyrwoman got impatient. "What happened? What
did Beterli say to you?" Keevan didn't want to say anything,
but finally he told her what happened. The Weyrwoman
160 smiled at Mende and left.

"Am I still a candidate?" Keevan asked Mende.

"Well, you are and you aren't, lovey," Mende said. "Is the
numbweed making the pain better?" Keevan nodded.

---

5. **Weyrwoman:** female leader of a Weyr.

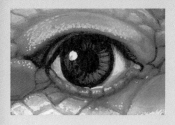

MAKING INFERENCES

Line 140 marks a sudden change of scene. Before, Keevan was fighting with Beterli. Now, it's the next morning, and Keevan is in bed. What happened?

_____

_____

_____

_____

_____

MAKING INFERENCES

Re-read lines 155–156. Why doesn't Keevan want to tell on Beterli? What does this say about Keevan's character?

_____

_____

_____

_____

_____

_____

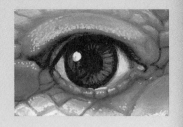

Your
TURN

MOTIVATION

In lines 189–195, why does Keevan want to give up? Why does he wish he had stayed in bed?

_____

_____

_____

_____

_____

At any other time, Keevan would have liked being taken
165 care of like this. But now he lay in bed worrying. Would the others think it was his fault? But everyone was there! Beterli had started the fight. Keevan's worry increased.

Eventually the numbweed made Keevan sleepy. He let go of his fears.

170 Then, he heard a hum. It began to grow. Keevan realized that the hatching had started. But he was flat in bed!

He sat up. The numbweed made it hard to move. Carefully, he took a step. The broken leg dragged. It hurt, but what was pain to a dragonman?

175 No one had said he couldn't go to the Impression. "You are and you aren't" were Mende's words.

The humming got louder and faster. Keevan knew he must hurry. But if he hurried down the ramp, he'd fall flat on his face.

180 He decided to go flat on his rear end, like a crawling child. Then he scrambled down the ramp. He waited a moment at the bottom to catch his breath. Somehow he managed to push himself up, even though he was dizzy.

Then he heard the crowd. He heard oohs, soft cheers, and
185 excited whispers. An egg had cracked, and the dragon had chosen his rider. Keevan went even faster. If he didn't get there soon, there'd be no hatchling left for him.

Finally, Keevan staggered onto the Hatching Ground. No one noticed him. And Keevan couldn't see anything but the
190 backs of the candidates. Suddenly, a large gap appeared in the wall of candidates, and Keevan saw the eggs. There didn't seem to be *any* left uncracked. He could see the lucky boys standing beside the dragons.

Suddenly he wished he'd stayed in bed. Now everyone
195 would see his shameful failure. So he scrambled to reach the shadowy walls of the Hatching Ground. He mustn't be seen.

He didn't notice, therefore, that the remaining boys began to come toward him. Keevan collapsed, sobbing, onto the sand. He didn't see how confused the Weyrfolk were. He 200 didn't hear the whispers of people guessing what would come next.

The Weyrleader and Weyrwoman had joined the crowd of boys moving toward the entrance.

"I've never seen anything like it," the Weyrleader was 205 saying. "Only thirty-nine riders chosen. And the bronze is trying to leave the Hatching Ground. It hasn't made an Impression yet!"

The Weyrwoman replied. "The hatchling makes no choice because the right boy isn't here."

210 "There's only Beterli and K'last's young son missing. And there's a full wing of likely boys to choose from. . . ."

"None are acceptable, it seems. Where is the dragon going? He's not going to the entrance after all. Oh, what is over there, in the shadows?"

215 Keevan heard the sounds of voices nearing him. He wanted to dig himself into the sand.

Don't worry! Please don't worry! The thought was urgent, but it wasn't his own.

Someone kicked sand over Keevan and knocked roughly 220 against him.

"Go away. Let me alone!" he cried.

Why? was the hurt-sounding question put in his mind. There was no voice, but the question was there. It was perfectly clear in his mind.

225 Keevan could not believe it. He lifted his head and stared into the glowing eyes of a small bronze dragon. The dragon was trying hard to stand up.

Keevan dragged himself to his knees. He wasn't aware of the pain in his legs. He didn't even see the ring of boys

Your TURN

VOCABULARY

You already know that a Weyrleader is a male leader of a Weyr, and a Weyrwoman is a female leader of a Weyr. Who are the Weyrfolk (line 199)?

_____

_____

_____

_____

_____

Your TURN

MAKING INFERENCES

Who is speaking in line 217? What clues on this page lead you to your inference? If you need another clue, re-read lines 16–19.

MAKING INFERENCES

Why do you think Heth chooses Keevan? Re-read Mende's opinion on the qualities dragons look for in a rider (lines 29–36). Then, look for clues in the story that show Keevan has these qualities. List two of these qualities and the clues that point to these qualities below.

1. Quality:

_____

_____

_____

Clue:

_____

_____

_____

2. Quality:

_____

_____

_____

Clue:

_____

_____

_____

230 who'd been passed over. Resentfully, they all watched him Impress the dragon. The Weyrfolk watched. They were amused and surprised at the dragon's choice.

Why? asked the dragon again. *Don't you like me?* His eyes showed fear. His voice was so sad that Keevan staggered
235 forward and threw his arms around the dragon's neck. Keevan stroked him and without words, he assured the hatchling over and over again that he was the most perfect, most beautiful, and most beloved dragon in all the Weyrs of Pern.

240 "What's his name, K'van?" asked Lessa, the Weyrwoman. She smiled warmly at the new dragonrider. Keevan stared at her for a while. Then he gave her a big smile. She had shortened his name, making him a dragonrider forever.

My name is Heth, the dragon thought. Then he hiccuped.
245 *I'm hungry.*

"Dragons are born hungry," said Lessa, laughing. F'lar, give the boy a hand. He can barely manage his own legs, much less a dragon's.

K'van remembered his stick and drew himself up. "We'll
250 be just fine, thank you."

"You may be the smallest dragonrider ever, young K'van," F'lar, the Weyrleader, said, "but you're one of the bravest!"

And Heth agreed! Heth's and K'van's hearts leaped with pride and joy. K'van wondered if his heart would burst right
255 out of his body. He looped an arm around Heth's neck. The pair, the smallest dragonboy and the hatchling who wouldn't choose anyone else, left together forever.

Making Inferences

Writers don't always tell you everything directly. Sometimes you need to guess what's happening or what a character is feeling. Don't make wild guesses, though! You can find clues in the text, put them together, and make an educated guess, or **inference.**

Inferences Web for "The Smallest Dragonboy"

Why is Beterli the way he is? You may need to do some guesswork to figure out what makes Beterli "tick." The diagram below can help you. First, find clues in the story that describe how Beterli acts, what he says, and how other people respond to him. Then, make your inference about Beterli based on these clues. Part of the diagram has been filled in for you.

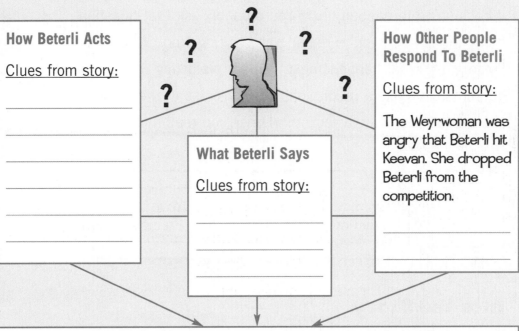

How Beterli Acts

Clues from story:

_____
_____
_____
_____
_____

What Beterli Says

Clues from story:

_____
_____
_____

How Other People Respond To Beterli

Clues from story:

The Weyrwoman was angry that Beterli hit Keevan. She dropped Beterli from the competition.

_____
_____

1. **Your Inference** about what Beterli is like:

   _____

2. *Why* do think Beterli is the way he is?

   _____

Antaeus

Literary Focus: Allusion

"Hey, I recognize Cinderella in this story!" Have you ever
had such a reaction when you're reading? If so, you may
have found an allusion. An **allusion** is a reference to another
story, character, place, or event. Writers often use allusions
to give their stories more depth. For example, the title of the
story you are about to read is an allusion to a character from
Greek mythology. Antaeus (an TEE uhs) is a giant whose
strength comes from his mother, the Earth. As long as his
feet are on the ground, Antaeus is all-powerful.

Reading Skill: Predicting

What's going to happen next? You probably ask that question
many times when you're reading an exciting story. When you
try to *guess* what happens next, you are **predicting** the
outcome. To make a prediction, look for clues in the story.
You can always change your mind once you read more and
find new clues!

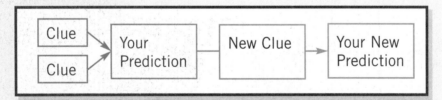

Into the Story

During World War II, the United States needed to make
equipment and weapons to serve the war effort. Since most
factories were in the North, many families left their homes
in the South to look for work. This is the situation the
narrator refers to as the story opens.

Antaeus

BASED ON THE STORY BY
Borden Deal

1　It was during the wartime. Lots of people were coming North for jobs in factories. Kids were sometimes thrown into new groups and new lives that were completely different from anything they had ever known before. I remember this one kid, T. J., who came from down South. His family moved 5　into our building.

Our building was just like all the others there. Families were crowded into a few rooms. There were about twenty-five or thirty kids about my age in that one building. Of course, there were a few of us who formed a gang. I was the 10　one who brought T. J. into the gang.

The building right next door to us was a factory. It was a low building with a flat, tarred roof. The roof had a wall all around it. No one paid any attention to the roof because it was higher than any of the other buildings around. So my 15　gang used the roof as a headquarters. We could get up there by crossing over to the fire escape from our own roof on a plank. It was a secret place for us.

I remember the day I first took T. J. up there to meet the gang. He was a healthy kid with lots of white hair. He talked 20　more slowly than any of us. You noticed the difference in the way he talked right away.

We climbed up over the wall and dropped down on the roof. The gang was there.

"Hi, " I said. I pointed to T. J. "He just moved into the 25　building yesterday." The gang said "Hi."

For a moment, no one had anything to say. T. J. looked around at the rooftop and down at the black tar under his feet. "Where I come from," he said, "we played out in the woods. Don't you have woods around here? Don't you have 30　fields to grow things in—no watermelons or anything?"

Adaptation of "Antaeus" by Borden Deal. Copyright © 1961 by Southern Methodist University Press. Retold by Holt, Rinehart and Winston. Reproduced by permission of **Ashley Deal Matin.**

"No," I said. "Why do you want to grow something? The folks can buy everything they need at the store."

He looked at me again with that strange look. "In Alabama," he said, "I had my own acre of cotton and my
35 own acre of corn. It was mine to plant and make every year."

Blackie said, "Who wants to have their own acre of cotton and corn? That's just work. What can you do with an acre of cotton and corn?"

T. J. explained, but we didn't understand anything. We
40 thought T. J. was strange and different. We were all attracted by his self-confidence.

He moved his foot against the black tar. "We could make our own field right here," he said softly. "When spring comes, we could grow watermelons."

45 "You'd have to be a good farmer to make these tar roofs grow any watermelons," I said. We all laughed.

But T. J. was serious. He said we could carry dirt up to the roof and spread it out even. We could water the seeds in the dirt. Then we'd have a crop.

50 I slapped T. J. on the shoulder. "That's a wonderful idea," I said. Everybody smiled at him. "Our own private roof garden." We decided that we would get the dirt from an empty lot near our school.

T. J. kept the project going all through the winter months.
55 He kept talking about the watermelons and the cotton we could grow. He got the other kids in the gang to help him carry the dirt to the roof after school.

When I think about it now, I don't see how he kept us on the project. It was hard work. We had to carry the boxes of
60 dirt all the way up the stairs to the roof. We also had to make sure no grown-ups saw what we were doing. But T. J. kept the vision bright within us.

Your
TURN

ALLUSION

Antaeus gets his strength from the earth. Which character in the story also gets his strength from the earth? Explain your answer below.

_____

_____

_____

_____

Your
TURN

PREDICTING

Do you think the garden will grow? Underline the clues in the story that lead you to your prediction. Explain your prediction below.

_____

_____

_____

_____

_____

During the cold months, the earth just lay there. It was lifeless. But one day it rained. After the rain there was a

65 softness to the air. The earth was alive and warm.

T. J. smelled the air. "It's spring," he said.

We all tried to sniff the air the way T. J. did. It was the first time in my life that spring and earth meant something to me. I looked at T. J. and understood the dream that lay

70 beyond his plan. He was a new Antaeus, preparing his own bed of strength.

"It's planting time," he said. "We'll have to find some seed."

"There are stores over on Sixth Street," I said. "We could

75 probably get some grass seed there."

T. J. looked at the earth and then at us. "You really want to grow some grass," he said. "I've never tried to grow grass."

"But it's pretty," Blackie said. "We could play on it. It's

80 like having our own lawn."

"Well," T. J. said. He looked at the rest of us. "I was thinking of growing vegetables. But we'll plant grass."

He was smart. He knew where to give in. And I don't think it made any difference to him. He just wanted to grow

85 something, even if it was grass.

"Of course," T. J. said. "I do think we should also plant a row of watermelons."

"All right," I said.

Things went very quickly then. We stole seed from the

90 open bins at the store. T. J. showed us how to prepare the earth and sow the grass seed. The earth looked rich and black with moisture. It seemed the grass grew overnight.

We couldn't walk or play on the grass as we had expected to. It was too delicate. But that was fine. It was enough to

95 look at the grass and realize that it was the work of our own
hands. We measured how much the grass grew each day.

T. J. was trying to find some watermelon seeds. He finally
got his hands on a seed catalog. "We can order them now,"
he said. "Look!" We all crowded around.

100 "What are you boys doing up here?" an adult voice said
behind us.

It surprised us. No one else had ever come up here before.
We turned around and saw three men. They weren't
policemen or night watchmen. They were three men in
105 business suits. They walked toward us.

"What are you boys doing up here?" the one in the middle
said again.

We stood still.

The men stared at the grass behind us. "What's this?" the
110 man said. "How did you get it up here?"

"We planted it," T. J. said.

The men kept looking at the grass as if they didn't believe
it. It was a thick carpet over the earth now.

"Yes, sir," T. J. said proudly. "We carried that earth up
115 here and planted that grass." He showed them the seed
catalog. "And we're planning to plant some watermelons."

The man look at him. "What do you think you're doing?
Do you want to go to jail?"

T. J. looked shaken. The rest of us were silent. We were
120 afraid of the men. We had grown up aware of adult authority.
We knew the power of policemen, night watchmen, and
teachers. This man sounded like all the others. But it was a
new thing to T. J.

One man said to another man beside him, "Make sure
125 that all that dirt is taken away tomorrow."

T. J. came forward. "That's our earth," he said. The man
looked at him coldly. "But it's my building."

Your TURN

PREDICTING

Did the garden grow? Were
you correct in your original
prediction? If not, which
new clues did you get that
made you change your
mind?

_____

_____

_____

_____

Your TURN

PREDICTING

Who are these men? Why
have they come to the roof?
What do you think will
happen now? Underline the
parts in the story that lead
you to your prediction.
Explain your prediction
below.

_____

_____

_____

_____

_____

Here's HOW

ALLUSION

Hey, I'm not sure T. J. is that similar to Antaeus after all. T. J. wasn't killed or anything! But then again, I see their fates are similar in other ways. When the garden is destroyed, T. J. can't live in the city anymore. T. J. can only feel alive—at home—when he connects to the earth.

The men walked away. T. J. stood and looked after them. He was angry.

130 He turned to us. "We won't let them do it," he said. "We'll stay up here all day tomorrow and the day after that. We won't let them do it."

We just looked at him. We knew there was no stopping the men. We started moving slowly to the fire escape.

135 "They can't touch it," T. J. said. "I won't let them lay a dirty hand on it!"

He picked up the dirt and threw it over the wall of the roof. We began to do the same. We destroyed the grass that we had grown.

140 It took less time than you would think. When it was finally over, we were all still. We looked down at the black tar. It felt harsh under the soles of our shoes.

T. J. stood for a moment. Then, he started moving to the fire escape.

145 We followed him. But T. J. was quick. He went down the fire escape and disappeared toward the street. He didn't look back.

They did not find him for two weeks.

Then the Nashville police caught him. He was walking
150 along the railroad track. He was heading South, heading home.

As for us, we never again climbed the fire escape to the roof.

Predicting

When you guess what happens next, you are **predicting** the outcome. The best thing about predicting is that you can always change your prediction (and often should) after you get new clues in the story.

Look back at the predictions you made while reading "Antaeus," and fill out this chart. First, write down clues in the story that led you to a specific prediction. Then, write your prediction. Next, write down new clues you found in the story. Finally, write your revised prediction, based on the new clues. Part of the chart has already been filled in for you.

1. Clue:

_____

_____

2. Clue:

_____

_____

My Prediction:

_____

_____

1. New Clue:

_____

_____

2. New Clue:

T. J. gives in to the boys and agrees to grow grass on the roof. The narrator says T. J. is smart.

My Revised Prediction:

_____

_____

The Highwayman

Literary Focus: Narrative Poems

Narrative poems tell a story. Like short stories, narrative poems have a **setting, characters, conflict, climax,** and **resolution.** Long ago, stories were sung to the music of a stringed instrument. Poems like "The Highwayman" use strong rhythms to make their stories sound like the old sung stories. Read the poem aloud to feel its galloping rhythm.

Subject vs. Theme

The **subject** of a story or poem is what it's about: love, war, skateboarding—you name it. A selection's **theme** is what it says about the subject.

Reading Skill: Make the Connection

As you read this poem, keep a piece of paper handy so that you can write down your reactions. Include your questions, your thoughts, and your feelings about the poem. Remember that you create your own meaning from "The Highwayman."

Into the Poem

"The Highwayman" is a narrative poem set in England in the 1700s. Highwaymen used to stop stagecoaches on deserted roads in England and Scotland. Then they robbed the rich passengers. Some of these robbers were romantic figures who wore elegant clothes. Others were heroes who shared the stolen money with the poor.

The
Highwayman

Alfred Noyes

PART 1

1   The wind was a torrent of darkness among the gusty trees,
    The moon was a ghostly galleon[1] tossed upon cloudy
        seas,
    The road was a ribbon of moonlight over the purple moor,
    And the highwayman came riding——
5   Riding——riding——
    The highwayman came riding, up to the old inn door.

> **IN OTHER WORDS**   In the moonlit night, a highway-
> man rode his horse through the dark countryside. Finally,
> he came to an old country inn.

    He'd a French cocked hat on his forehead, a bunch of
        lace at his chin,
    A coat of the claret[2] velvet, and breeches of brown
        doeskin.
    They fitted with never a wrinkle. His boots were up to the
        thigh.
10 And he rode with a jeweled twinkle,
        His pistol butts a-twinkle,
    His rapier hilt[3] a-twinkle, under the jeweled sky.

> **IN OTHER WORDS**   His clothes were elegant, and
> they fit perfectly. His guns and sword had jewels on their
> handles.

    Over the cobbles he clattered and clashed in the dark inn
        yard.
    And he tapped with his whip on the shutters, but all was

---

1. **galleon:** large sailing ship.
2. **claret** (KLAR uht): purplish red, like claret wine.
3. **rapier** (RAY pee uhr) **hilt:** sword handle.

Here's HOW

NARRATIVE POEM

In lines 1–6, I can see the setting in my mind. It's night, and there is a moon and a few clouds, too. The moon lights up the road in the dark countryside. A robber is riding down the road. (He's got to be on a horse. It's the 1700s.) I can hear the clop-clop of the horse's hooves. He rides up to an old inn.

Your TURN

NARRATIVE POEM

In lines 7–9, circle five items of clothing the highwayman is wearing. Then, on the lines below, tell whether you think he is dressed well or poorly.

_____

_____

Here's HOW

SUBJECT VS. THEME

The title of the poem is "The Highwayman." Lines 7–11 describe him. He must be the subject of the poem.

locked and barred.

15 He whistled a tune to the window, and who should be
    waiting there

But the landlord's black-eyed daughter,
    Bess, the landlord's daughter,
Plaiting⁴ a dark red love knot into her long black hair.

And dark in the dark old inn yard a stable wicket⁵ creaked

20 Where Tim the ostler⁶ listened. His face was white and
    peaked.

His eyes were hollows of madness, his hair like moldy
    hay,

But he loved the landlord's daughter,
    The landlord's red-lipped daughter,
Dumb as a dog he listened, and he heard the robber say——

25 "One kiss, my bonny sweetheart, I'm after a prize tonight,
But I shall be back with the yellow gold before the
    morning light;
Yet, if they press me sharply, and harry⁷ me through the
    day,

---

4. **plaiting:** braiding.
5. **wicket:** small door or gate.
6. **ostler** (AHS luhr): person who takes care of horses; groom.
7. **harry:** harass or push along.

Here's
HOW

MAKE THE CONNECTION

In line 20, a new character comes in. Tim, the guy who takes care of the horses, is behind the gate, listening to the highwayman's plans. He's in love with the girl, too. What's he doing sneaking around at midnight? I'll bet he's jealous and will make trouble.

Your
TURN

NARRATIVE POEM

In lines 19–24, underline three phrases or sentences that describe Tim's appearance.

Your
TURN

VOCABULARY

The word *stable* can mean "steady and strong," "likely to last," "the racehorses owned by one person," or "a building for horses." What does the word *stable* mean in line 19?

_____

_____

Your TURN

VOCABULARY

The words *cascade* and *waves* are used in lines 33–34. You can figure out the meaning of those two words by reading lines 32–34 again. Circle the word that gives you the clue to the meaning of the words.

Then look for me by moonlight,

Watch for me by moonlight,

30 I'll come to thee by moonlight, though hell should bar the

way."

IN OTHER WORDS The highwayman told his girlfriend that he was going to rob another stagecoach that night. He planned to come back that same night, but the soldiers might give him trouble. If so, then he would be back the next night.

He rose upright in the stirrups.[8] He scarce could reach

her hand,

But she loosened her hair in the casement.[9] His face

burnt like a brand

As the black cascade of perfume came tumbling over his

breast;

And he kissed its waves in the moonlight,

35   (Oh, sweet black waves in the moonlight!)

Then he tugged at his rein[10] in the moonlight, and galloped

away to the west.

IN OTHER WORDS He tried to kiss her goodbye, but the window was too high. So she let her hair down, and he kissed it. Then, he rode off.

PART 2

He did not come in the dawning. He did not come at

noon;

And out of the tawny sunset, before the rise of the moon,

---

8. stirrups: foot supports attached to a horse saddle.
9. casement: window that opens outward on hinges.
10. rein: strap attached to bit in mouth to control a horse.

When the road was a gypsy's ribbon, looping the purple
    moor,
40 A redcoat troop came marching——
    Marching——marching——
King George's men came marching, up to the old inn
    door.

> **IN OTHER WORDS**   He didn't come back that night,
> and he didn't show up the next day. However, soldiers
> came to the inn.

They said no word to the landlord. They drank his ale
    instead.
But they gagged his daughter, and bound her, to the foot of
    her narrow bed.
45 Two of them knelt at her casement, with muskets at their
    side!
There was death at every window;
    And hell at one dark window;
For Bess could see, through her casement, the road that
    he would ride.

> **IN OTHER WORDS**   The soldiers drank the
> innkeeper's beer. They also tied his daughter to the foot
> of her bed. Two soldiers with guns watched out her
> window for the highwayman.

They had tied her up to attention, with many a sniggering
    jest;[11]
50 They had bound a musket[12] beside her, with the muzzle
    beneath her breast!

---

11. **sniggering jest:** a snickered joke.
12. **musket:** a gun used by soldiers.

THE HIGHWAYMAN **63**

Here's HOW

MAKE THE CONNECTION

What's happening in lines 37–42? The highwayman doesn't come back when he's supposed to. He was too much in love with that girl to just leave. Uh-oh. There's something about the way the author repeats *marching* that seems threatening. I'm guessing that the guy's in trouble or he's going to be in trouble soon.

Your TURN

VOCABULARY

The word *muzzle* can mean "the nose and jaws of an animal," "a mouth covering used to keep an animal from biting or eating," "to gag or force silence," or "the open end of a gun." What do you think *muzzle* means in line 50?

_____

_____

_____

Your TURN

MAKE THE CONNECTION

Who is the dead man referred to in line 51? Why is he called a dead man?

_____

_____

_____

_____

_____

_____

Here's HOW

MAKE THE CONNECTION

Not very much is going on here. In line 57, it even says that the time was just crawling. Maybe the author wants me to feel that time is passing slowly. Then all of a sudden, Bess reaches the trigger. She does it just at midnight. That gives me chills. The exact time somehow makes the little thing she did seem exciting.

"Now, keep good watch!" and they kissed her. She heard
 the dead man say——
Look for me by moonlight;
Watch for me by moonlight;
I'll come to thee by moonlight, though hell should bar the
 way!

IN OTHER WORDS The soldiers had tied the innkeeper's daughter so that a gun was pointed at her chest. They teased her and kissed her and told her to watch for the highwayman. She knew he was riding into a death trap.

55 She twisted her hands behind her; but all the knots held
 good!
She writhed[13] her hands till her fingers were wet with
 sweat or blood!
They stretched and strained in the darkness, and the hours
 crawled by like years,
Till, now, on the stroke of midnight,
 Cold, on the stroke of midnight,
60 The tip of one finger touched it! The trigger at least was
 hers!

IN OTHER WORDS She tried for hours to loosen the ropes, but they were very tight. Finally, at midnight, she could reach the trigger of the gun.

The tip of one finger touched it; she strove[14] no more for
 the rest!
Up, she stood up to attention, with the muzzle beneath

---

13. **writhed** (RYTHD): twisted back and forth.
14. **strove**: past tense of *strive;* try hard.

her breast.
She would not risk their hearing; she would not strive
again;
For the road lay bare in the moonlight;
65   Blank and bare in the moonlight;
And the blood of her veins, in the moonlight, throbbed to
her love's refrain.

IN OTHER WORDS   She had reached the trigger. That was all she needed. She didn't want the soldiers to know what she had done. She watched the road for the highwayman.

Tlot-tlot; tlot-tlot! Had they heard it? The horse hoofs
ringing clear;
Tlot-tlot, tlot-tlot, in the distance? Were they deaf that they
did not hear?
Down the ribbon of moonlight, over the brow of the hill,
70   The highwayman came riding,
Riding, riding!
The redcoats looked to their priming![15] She stood up,
straight and still.

IN OTHER WORDS   She heard the highwayman coming on his horse. The soldiers got their guns ready. She stood up.

Tlot-tlot, in the frosty silence! *Tlot-tlot,* in the echoing
night!
Nearer he came and nearer. Her face was like a light!
75   Her eyes grew wide for a moment; she drew one last
deep breath,

---

15. **priming:** explosive for firing a gun.

NARRATIVE POEM

In lines 67–68, circle the repeated words the author uses to build rhythm and create excitement in the poem.

SUBJECT VS. THEME

This poem is definitely not just about the highwayman. Bess is in it more than he is. It's about the love between them, too.

Then her fingers moved in the moonlight,
    Her musket shattered the moonlight,
Shattered her breast in the moonlight and warned
    him——with her death.

IN OTHER WORDS   The highwayman came nearer. She took a deep breath and pulled the trigger. The shot killed her, but it warned him, as she had planned.

He turned. He spurred to the west; he did not know who
    stood
80 Bowed, with her head o'er the musket, drenched with her
    own blood!
Not till the dawn he heard it, his face grew gray to hear
How Bess, the landlord's daughter,
    The landlord's black-eyed daughter,
Had watched for her love in the moonlight, and died in the
    darkness there.

IN OTHER WORDS   The highwayman quickly turned around and rode in the other direction. He didn't hear until dawn that his girlfriend had shot herself to warn him.

85 Back, he spurred like a madman, shouting a curse to the
    sky,
With the white road smoking behind him and his rapier
    brandished high.
Blood-red were his spurs in the golden noon; wine-red was
    his velvet coat;
When they shot him down on the highway,
    Down like a dog on the highway,
90 And he lay in his blood on the highway, with the bunch of
    lace at his throat.

IN OTHER WORDS   He rode back like a madman, cursing. The soldiers shot him on the highway. He lay there in his own blood, still in his fine clothes.

And still of a winter's night, they say, when the wind is in
  the trees,
When the moon is a ghostly galleon tossed upon cloudy
  seas,
When the road is a ribbon of moonlight over the purple
  moor,
A highwayman comes riding——
95   *Riding——riding——*
A highwayman comes riding, up to the old inn door.

Over the cobbles he clatters and clangs in the dark inn yard;
He taps with his whip on the shutters, but all is locked and
  barred.
He whistles a tune to the window, and who should be
  waiting there
100 *But the landlord's black-eyed daughter,*
  Bess, the landlord's daughter,
Plaiting a dark red love knot into her long black hair.

IN OTHER WORDS   The legend of Bess and the highwayman lives on. On some winter nights when the moon is up and the wind blows, the ghost of the highwayman rides again. He rides to the inn and knocks on the window. The innkeeper's daughter is still waiting for him and is still braiding her hair.

Your TURN

MAKE THE CONNECTION

Lines 91–102 look different from the rest of the poem. How do these lines make you feel? Do you like the way the poem ends?

_____
_____
_____
_____

Your TURN

SUBJECT VS. THEME

What does the poem say about its subject, the love between the highwayman and Bess?

_____
_____
_____
_____
_____
_____

Story Map

"The Highwayman" is a **narrative poem** about love, betrayal, and death. Fill in the boxes in this story map to show the main parts of the story. Some of the information has been filled in for you.

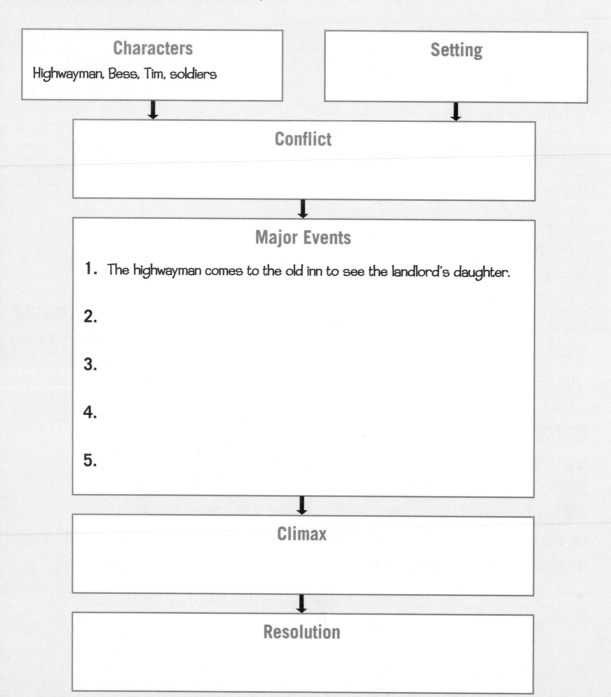

Characters	Setting
Highwayman, Bess, Tim, soldiers	

Conflict

Major Events

1. The highwayman comes to the old inn to see the landlord's daughter.

2.

3.

4.

5.

Climax

Resolution

Vocabulary

Match each word in the Word Bank at right with its correct definition below. Write the matching word on the blank in front of the correct definition. Then, use the word in a sentence of your own. Write your sentence on the blank lines after the definition. The first one has been done for you.

1. _____brandished_____ waved or shaken in a threatening way

The highwayman brandished his sword as he rode down the road.

2. _____ unable or unwilling to speak

3. _____ a repeated phrase in a song or poem

4. _____ a mark on the skin made from burning iron

5. _____ looking pale, as from an illness

Gentlemen of the Road

Reading Skill: Cause and Effect

Have you ever seen someone knock over a row of dominoes? This is a good example of **cause and effect.** The person knocks over only one domino. The first domino knocks over the next one, and so on, until they've all fallen over. Knocking over the first domino is a **cause.** A cause makes something happen. What happens is called an **effect.** Each effect can then also become a cause. The second domino falling over is an effect. It becomes a cause, though, when it knocks over the third domino.

This chart shows how one effect becomes a cause for another effect.

Cause: Some people in England became very rich.

↓

Effect (and New Cause): The government built toll roads for these rich people to travel on.

↓

Effect:

Into the Article

Over the years, the definition of *gentleman* has changed. Originally, a gentleman was someone from the wealthy upper class. Upper-class people tended to be very polite to each other. Today, anyone who behaves politely might be called a gentleman, whether he is rich or not.

Gentlemen

of the Road

Based on the Article by

Mara Rockliff

1   Highwaymen (like Bess's beloved)[1] were bandits. They robbed travelers in seventeenth- and eighteenth-century England. Why did people once think of them as gentlemen?

Many people in England became rich in those centuries.
5   The rich dressed in silks and velvets. They lived in huge houses. They traveled to London for parties. They spent summers by the sea. But the poor lived in filth. In the worst years, 74 percent of the children in London died before the age of five.

10   New toll roads ran through the countryside. Rich people traveled on these good roads. The highwaymen could stop travelers and rob them.

The highwaymen called themselves gentlemen of the road. How did they get this reputation?

15   Some people saw them as Robin Hoods. (They gave some of what they stole to the poor.)

These bandits looked like gentlemen. Many began poor. But once they got money, they dressed in style.

Some highwaymen tried to act like gentlemen as well.
20   They were polite to ladies. They sometimes asked their victims' forgiveness. Some bandits let their victims keep precious items. Others took only what they felt they needed and returned the rest.

Even when caught and sentenced to hang, some
25   highwaymen acted bravely. They did not cry or beg for mercy. With the noose around their necks, some threw themselves off the scaffold. They did not wait for the wagon they stood on to be pulled from under them. In songs and stories, this last act made them look brave in the face of
30   death.

---

1. like Bess's beloved: This reference is to Alfred Noyes' poem "The Highwayman." Bess was the innkeeper's daughter. She loved a highwayman.

Cause-and-Effect Chart

The graphic organizer below can be used to collect information about causes and effects. Fill in the boxes as you re-read the article "Gentlemen of the Road." The first cause and the last effect have been done for you.

Cause: Some people in England became very rich.

⬇

Effect:

⬇

Effect:

⬇

Effect:

⬇

Effect: Robbers began behaving like the rich gentlemen they were robbing.

The Fall of the House of Poe?

Reading Skill: Taking Notes and Outlining

When you take notes, you look for the main ideas in a selection. Each part of a story, article, or essay may have a main idea. If you put all these main ideas together, you should be able to come up with an overall main idea.

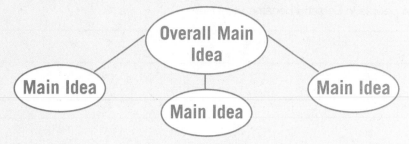

Note main ideas and supporting details in outline form. When you finish a section of the article that has a main idea, write down notes following a main idea–details formula:

> **Main Idea**
>
> Earthquake caused damage in Alaska.
>
> **Supporting Details**
>
> —roads blocked
> —houses split in two
> —earth split open

Note: A supporting detail usually answers the question **Why?** or **How?** about the main idea.

Into the Article

"The Fall of the House of Usher" is a Poe story about a house's downfall. This article is about people wanting to tear down a house that other people think should be saved.

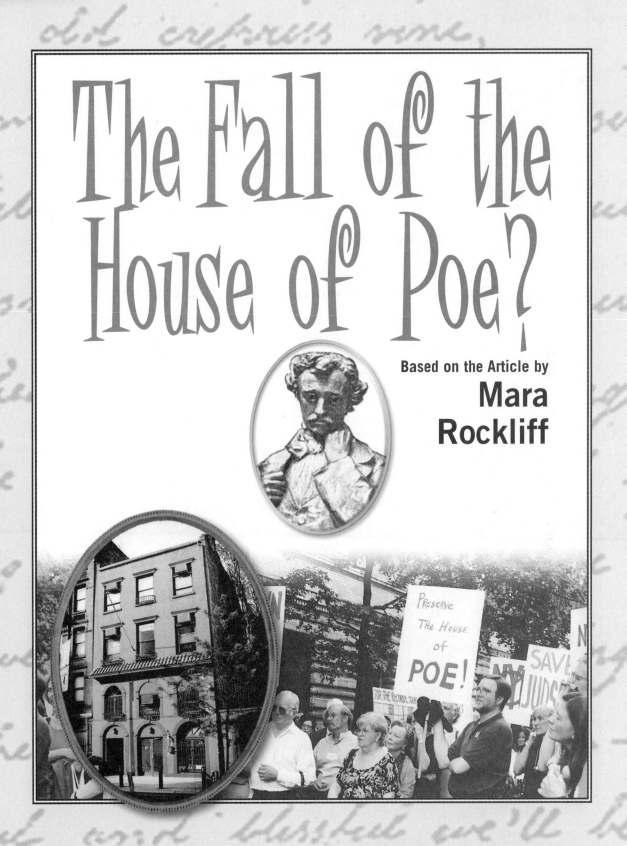

The Fall of the House of Poe?

Based on the Article by
Mara Rockliff

Here's
HOW

TAKING NOTES

The main idea of lines 1–9 is that New York University wants to tear down a building that Edgar Allan Poe once lived in.

Your
TURN

TAKING NOTES

What is the main idea of lines 13–16? Underline the supporting details.

_____

_____

_____

_____

_____

_____

Your
TURN

VOCABULARY

The word *appeal* can mean "charm," "interest," "apply to a higher court," or "request." Which meaning do you think *appeal* has in line 28?

_____

_____

_____

1 **H**ow would you feel if your favorite place were torn down? Terrible, right?

If Edgar Allan Poe were alive today, he might feel terrible about the loss of a boardinghouse[1] where he once lived in
5 New York City. Some people want to tear it down.

New York University now owns the building. For years it has held classrooms and offices. But in 1999, NYU officials decided to tear it down. A new law school building would replace it.

10 Loyal Poe fans objected. They wrote letters. They passed around petitions. At a rally, hundreds of people chanted, "No, no, Poe won't go."

NYU representatives said Poe had lived in the boardinghouse for as little as six months. He had written no
15 important works there. One spokesperson for NYU said, "This is not a building that remembers Poe."

Eight other buildings where Poe lived in New York City are gone. Protesters found he and his wife had lived in this one the longest. Those months may have been his
20 happiest. He was at the top of his career. He was writing and editing his own magazine. He also had published *The Raven and Other Poems*.

On September 29, 2000, after checking all the facts, State Supreme Court Judge Robert E. Lippmann dismissed
25 the case. He found no legal reason to stop NYU from tearing down the Poe house. An NYU spokesman added, "The Tell-Tale Heart does not beat beneath the floorboards of this building." Preservation groups planned to appeal the judge's decision.

---

1. boardinghouse: a house where people live and pay for their rooms and meals.

Main-Idea Outline

Improve your understanding of "The Fall of the House of Poe?" by taking notes as you re-read the article. Fill in the outline below with the main ideas and supporting details from the text. Then, review your notes to come up with a statement of the main idea for the entire article. The first part of the outline has been done for you.

Main Idea 1:

NYU wants to tear down a building that Edgar Allan Poe lived in.

Supporting Details:

-NYU wants to build a law school building in its place

Main Idea 4:

_____

_____

Supporting Details:

_____

_____

Main Idea 2:

_____

_____

Supporting Details:

_____

_____

Main Idea 5:

_____

_____

Supporting Details:

_____

_____

Main Idea 3:

_____

_____

Supporting Details:

_____

_____

Overall Main Idea

_____

_____

_____

_____

It Just Keeps Going and Going . . .

Reading Skill: Cause and Effect

This article uses **cause and effect.** The author describes a series, or chain, of causes and effects. Each event **causes** another event to happen. The event it causes is called an **effect.**

Weather events are good examples of cause and effect. When hot air hits cold air, rain is the effect.

Writers use certain words to help show cause and effect. These words show how one event is connected to another. The chart below contains some common cause-and-effect words.

Cause-and-Effect Words	
• after	• for this reason
• as a result	• since
• because	• so
• consequently	• so that
• for	• then
	• therefore

Into the Article

This article explains how computer viruses work. It uses a model to help explain. A teacher throws away an incorrect answer key. Unfortunately, he misses the wastebasket. Later, the cleaner thinks the teacher threw the answer key away by mistake. This error causes a chain of causes and effects. The simple mistake causes a very big mess.

It just keeps Going and Going . . .

Based on the Article by

Joan Burditt

CAUSE AND EFFECT

I think I understand cause and effect. In lines 12–14, the teacher missed the wastebasket, and the answer key fell on the floor. That caused the cleaner to think it wasn't trash. If the teacher had picked up the paper, the problem wouldn't have happened. Not doing something right can cause effects you never imagine.

Your
TURN

CAUSE AND EFFECT

The answer key was only one cause of the problems. In lines 11–21, underline another cause of the problems.

1 **I**t is a human-made monster. No one can escape it. It can reach around the entire planet. This monster is called the Brain, Crusher, Grog, and the Creeper. It reproduces fast. It shuts down entire systems. It's a computer virus.

5 Experts disagree on how serious these viruses really are. In fact, information and opinions on viruses are spreading as fast as the viruses themselves. Viruses are self-replicating. That means they make copies of themselves over and over.

A model by computer scientist Eugene Kaspersky shows
10 how a computer virus works.

A teacher finds mistakes in an exam answer key. So he tosses it at the trash can and leaves. Later, a
15 cleaner sees the answer key on the floor. He puts it back on the desk. A sticky note is now stuck to the key. The note says, "Copy two
20 times, and put copies in other teachers' boxes."

The next day, the teacher calls in sick. A substitute takes over for the teacher. She sees the answer key

25　with the note stuck to it. She leaves the note on. Then, she copies and passes out the answer key.

The other teachers give the

30　key and note to the office clerk. She then makes more copies and passes them out. By the end of the day, the school is out of paper. The teachers' boxes are filled

35　with useless answer keys.

- -

This example shows what happens with a computer virus. The difference between the model and a computer virus is in the intent. The teacher didn't plan to create a monster. The whole mess was just a series of causes and effects. On the

40　other hand, people create computer viruses to cause trouble. The virus destroys correct information. It costs billions of dollars in lost work time every year.

People working on antivirus programs are making it easier to find a virus before it spreads. Still, watch what you

45　put in your computer . . . and in your trash.

Here's
HOW

CAUSE AND EFFECT

I can see that there was another *cause* of the problem. The regular teacher was sick the day after he threw the answer key at the trash can. His absence caused a substitute teacher to come to school. If he had not been sick, he would have thrown the answer key back in the trash. The problem would not have happened.

Your
TURN

CAUSE AND EFFECT

What **effect** did the substitute teacher create?

_____

_____

_____

_____

_____

Cause-and-Effect Chart

After you read "It Just Keeps Going and Going . . . ," re-read the part about the teachers. Find the causes and effects in that part. Then, record the causes and effects in the chart below. The first one has been done for you.

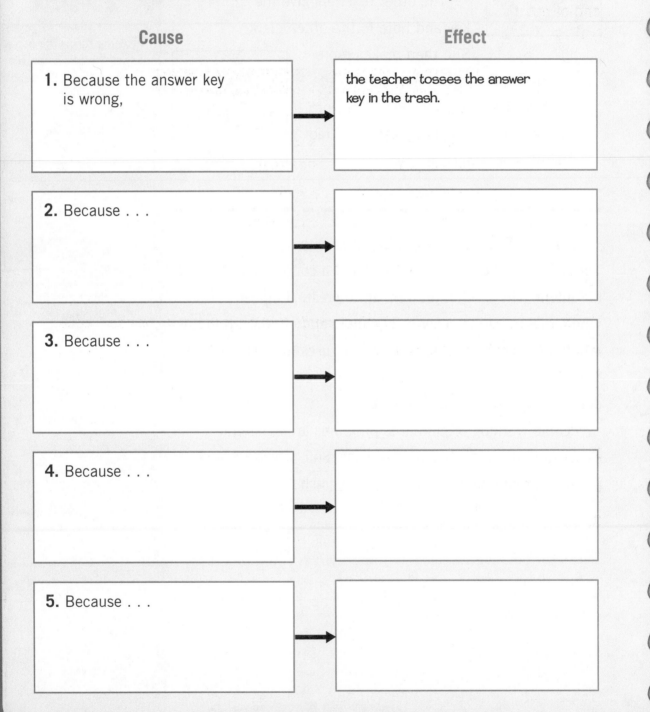

Cause	Effect
1. Because the answer key is wrong,	the teacher tosses the answer key in the trash.
2. Because . . .	
3. Because . . .	
4. Because . . .	
5. Because . . .	

Cause and Effect

Certain words and phrases show how one idea is connected to another. These words and phrases also help make clear the relationships between causes and effects. The chart below lists some of the words and phrases that show cause and effect.

Cause-and-Effect Words and Phrases	
• after	• since
• as a result	• so
• because	• so that
• consequently	• then
• for	• therefore
• for this reason	

Choose three of the cause-and-effect words and phrases from the chart above and write a sentence for each.

1. _____

_____

2. _____

_____

3. _____

_____

Echo and Narcissus

Literary Focus: Recurring Themes

Who am I? How should I live my life? People all over the world have basically the same dreams, fears, and questions about life. That's why the same themes come up again and again—or recur—in the stories people tell. These common themes are called **recurring themes.**

Reading Skill: Context Clues

As you read, you often see words that you do not know. Sometimes, you can figure out what a word means by looking at the words around it—the **context.** Look in a dictionary to see if you are right. You may find it helpful to make a chart like this one.

New Word	Clues from the Text	Word's Meaning	Dictionary Check
furious	Hera thought of a fitting punishment.	very angry	Correct!

Into the Myth

The ancient Greeks believed in dozens of mythical gods and other creatures, such as nymphs (nimpfs). This story is about a nymph named Echo and a young man named Narcissus (nahr SIHS uhs). The story is an origin myth because it explains how two things came into the world. This story was first told thousands of years ago, and the names *Echo* and *Narcissus* have become common words.

Based on the Myth Retold by
Roger Lancelyn Green

Echo and Narcissus

Here's
HOW

CONTEXT CLUES

In lines 10–12, the context for the word *detaining* (line 11) is that Echo is telling Hera many stories and gossipy tales. *Detaining* probably means "stopping" or "holding back." A check in the dictionary shows I am right.

Your
TURN

CONTEXT CLUES

Underline the words in lines 22–23 that give the context for the word *scorned*. What do you think *scorned* (line 22) means? Write your answer on the lines below. Then, check your answer in a dictionary.

_____

_____

_____

1 Echo was one of many nymphs, or fairies, who lived in the Greek mountains. She was very beautiful, but she always talked too much. Once she made Hera,[1] queen of the gods, very angry.

5 Here's what happened. Zeus,[2] king of the gods, lived on Mount Olympus with the other gods. Sometimes Zeus descended from Olympus to spend time on earth with the nymphs. That made Hera, his wife, jealous. She would come down to earth to search for him.

10 Each time, Hera met Echo, who talked on and on and on. Finally, Hera realized that Echo was purposely detaining her with endless stories and gossip. While Echo talked, Zeus hurried back to Mount Olympus. He pretended he'd been there all along.

15 Furious with Echo, Hera thought of a fitting punishment. "From now on," she commanded, "you can only repeat what others say. You will never be able to speak first."

Echo wept at her cruel punishment. She was sad and
20 lonely, but soon she had another misfortune. She fell in love with a handsome young hunter named Narcissus.

Many nymphs loved Narcissus, but he scorned them all. He loved only himself.

When Echo saw Narcissus, she fell madly in love. Since
25 she could not speak, she followed him secretly.

One day Narcissus became lost. "Is anybody here?" he called.

---

1. **Hera** (HIRH uh).
2. **Zeus** (ZOOS).

"Narcissus" (retitled "Echo and Narcissus") adapted from *Tales the Muses Told* by Roger Lancelyn Green. Copyright © 1965 by Richard G. Lancelyn-Green. Published by The Bodley Head. Retold by Holt, Rinehart and Winston. Reproduced by permission of **Random House UK Ltd.**

Echo repeated, "Here!"

Narcissus looked around but saw no one. "Whoever you

30 are, come to me!"

And Echo responded, "Come to me!"

Whatever he said, Echo repeated. Then, he cried, "Let us meet!"

Happily, she came running from her hiding place. When

35 she tried to hug him, he shoved her away. He told her he would rather die than have her touch him.

"I would have you touch me!" poor Echo repeated.

"I'll never let you kiss me," he told her.

"Kiss me! Kiss me!" Echo sank to the ground.

40 Narcissus hurried away. "Kissing you would kill me!" he called back furiously.

"Kill me!" Echo begged. Her heart was broken.

Aphrodite,[3] goddess of love, granted Echo's wish. Echo pined away and died. But we can still hear her voice among

45 the rocks when someone calls.

Aphrodite decided to punish Narcissus. He had insulted her by scorning Echo and the other nymphs. "He shall love only himself and die," she said.

One day Narcissus came to a pool in the mountains.

50 Thirsty, he lay down to drink.

He was surprised to see a beautiful face in the water looking up at him. He thought it was a water nymph and fell immediately in love.

"I love you! Be mine!" he cried.

55 But when he reached into the water, the face disappeared. When the water grew still again, his beloved's face returned.

Narcissus had no idea he was seeing his own reflection.

3. **Aphrodite** (af ruh DYT ee).

Here's HOW

CONTEXT CLUES

In lines 42–45, Echo is really sad that Narcissus doesn't love her. She says she wants to die. The context tells me that the word *pined* (line 44) probably has something to do with sadness and dying. The dictionary says it means "to waste away through grief or longing," so I am right.

Your TURN

CONTEXT CLUES

Re-read lines 58–64. What do you think *enchanted* (line 61) means? Write your answer on the lines below. Then, check your answer in a dictionary.

_____

_____

Narcissus thought he was so pretty. He couldn't look at anyone but himself. So, a goddess turned him into a flower. I think one theme of this myth is that you can't love other people when you are too involved in yourself.

Your
TURN

RECURRING THEMES

A recurring theme in literature is that love is stronger than death. Re-read lines 70–71. Then, tell how Narcissus's and Echo's loves "outlive" death.

_____

_____

_____

_____

_____

_____

(Maybe it was the first time a pool reflected the face of
60 someone looking into it.)

He was enchanted and couldn't leave. Helplessly, he lay each day gazing at his beloved's face. Like Echo, he could not have the love he wanted. He, too, pined away and died from a broken heart.

65 His last words were, "Farewell, my love, farewell." Whispering, Echo repeated them.

In the spring, a new flower appeared where Narcissus had died. It was the first narcissus—with white petals around a yellow center.

70 And so we know why there are echoes and how the first narcissus flower came to be.

Context-Clues Chart

Complete the following context-clues chart. For each word, write the clues from the nearby text. Then, write what you think the word means. Finally, look in a dictionary to see if you were right. The first word has been done for you.

New Word	Clues from the Text	Word's Meaning	Dictionary Check
1. *detaining* (line 11)	Echo "talked on and on," telling "endless stories."	holding back	Correct!
2. *scorned* (line 22)			
3. *pined* (line 44)			
4. *enchanted* (line 61)			

After Twenty Years

Literary Focus: Omniscient Point of View

"Who's telling this story?" This is a good question to ask when you start reading. When you do this, you're asking about **point of view.**

"After Twenty Years" is told from the **omniscient point of view.** An omniscient narrator knows everything about all the characters. When you read O. Henry's story, think about what important information the omniscient narrator knows but chooses not to tell us.

Reading Skill: Making Predictions

Part of the fun of reading is guessing what will happen next. When we do this, we are **making predictions.** Here's how to make predictions.

Clue	Prediction	New Prediction
Look for clues that hint at what's next. →	Predict possible outcomes. →	Revise predictions as you read more.

Into the Story

"After Twenty Years" is a short story with a surprise ending. It takes place in New York in the early 1900s. Two men who were childhood friends agree to meet at a certain place and time. They haven't seen each other for twenty years. One man had gone to seek his fortune in the West. The other didn't want to leave New York. As you read, look for clues in the men's words and appearances that tell what kind of man each is. Can you guess what the surprise ending will be?

After Twenty Years

Based on the Story by

O. Henry

1 The policeman walked up the street. He always walked boldly.

There were few people out that night. It was too cold, windy, and rainy.

5 The officer studied the street carefully. With his strong body and bold walk, he could turn heads. Lights were on at a few stores. Most stores had been closed for hours, though.

The policeman slowed down. A man leaned against the
10 doorway of a dark hardware store. He had an unlit cigar in his mouth.

"It's all right, Officer," he said quickly. "I'm just waiting for a friend. We decided to meet here twenty years ago. There used to be a restaurant here."

15 "It was torn down five years ago," said the policeman.

The man struck a match and lit his cigar. The light showed a pale face with a square jaw. He had a little white scar near his right eyebrow. He wore a large diamond pin in his scarf.

20 "Twenty years ago tonight," said the man, "I ate here with Jimmy Wells. We were raised together here in New York. We were like brothers. The next morning, I was leaving for the West to make my fortune. Jimmy didn't want to leave New York. We agreed to meet here in twenty
25 years."

The policeman said, "Twenty years is a long time. Haven't you heard from your friend?"

"Well, yes, we wrote for a time," said the man. "But after a year or two, we stopped. The West is a big place,
30 and I kept moving around. I know Jimmy will meet me if he's alive."

The man pulled out a watch. It was decorated with small diamonds.

"Three minutes to ten," he said. "It was exactly ten
35 o'clock when we left here twenty years ago."

"Did pretty well out West, didn't you?" asked the policeman.

"You bet! I hope Jimmy has done half as well. He was a good man—a bit slow, though. It takes the West to make a
40 man really sharp."

"I'll be leaving," said the policeman. "I hope your friend comes soon. Are you going to leave if he's not here by ten?"

"No!" said the other. "I'll give him at least half an
45 hour. If he's alive, he will be here by then. Goodbye, Officer."

"Good night, sir," said the policeman.

A light, cold rain fell. The wind had increased. The man smoked and waited for his friend.

50 In about twenty minutes, a tall man crossed the street. He was wearing a long coat with the collar turned up to his ears. He went directly to the man in the door.

"Is that you, Bob?" he asked.

"Is that you, Jimmy Wells?" cried the man in the door.

55 "Bless my heart!" said the tall man.

He grasped Bob's hands. "I was sure you'd come. Twenty years is a long time! The old restaurant is gone, Bob. How has the West treated you, old man?"

"Very well. I have everything I ever wanted. You've
60 changed a lot, Jimmy. You seem two or three inches taller."

"Oh, I grew a bit after I was twenty."

"Are you doing well in New York, Jimmy?"

"Okay. I work for the city. Come on, Bob. We'll go to a place I know and have a long talk about old times."

Your
TURN

MAKING PREDICTIONS

In lines 38–40, the man in the doorway boasts about how well he has done. On the lines below, write what you think will happen to him.

_____

_____

_____

_____

Your
TURN

MAKING PREDICTIONS

Make a prediction about the clue underlined in line 60.

_____

_____

_____

_____

_____

Here's
HOW

MAKING PREDICTIONS

In lines 65–67, Bob is doing most of the talking about his success. The other man is just listening. Could that mean the other man didn't do too well? Is he jealous of the success of Bob? Ah! I'll bet he thinks Bob got rich illegally!

Your TURN

MAKING PREDICTIONS

In lines 71–75, a sentence lets the reader accurately predict the conclusion of the story. Underline that sentence.

Your TURN

OMNISCIENT POINT OF VIEW

Why do you think O. Henry chose to tell his story from the omniscient point of view? What might the story have been like if it were told from Jimmy's point of view?

65   The two men walked up the street, arm in arm. The man from the West talked a lot about his success. The other man listened with interest.

A brightly lit drugstore stood at the corner. When they came into the light, each man turned to look at the other's

70   face.

The man from the West stopped suddenly. He released his arm.

"You're not Jimmy Wells," he snapped. "Even twenty years can't change a man's nose from a Roman to a pug."[1]

75   "It sometimes changes a good man into a bad one," said the tall man. "You've been under arrest for ten minutes, 'Silky' Bob. The police department in Chicago thought you might have come here. They want to talk to you. Before we go to the station, here's a note I was asked to give you. It's

80   from Patrolman Wells."

The man from the West unfolded the little piece of paper. By the time he had read the note, his hand shook.

Bob: I was at the place on time. When you struck the match to light your cigar, I saw it was the face of the

85   man wanted in Chicago. Somehow I couldn't arrest you myself. Instead, I went around and got a plainclothes man to do the job.

Jimmy

---

1. "*. . . change a man's nose from a Roman to a pug.*": A Roman nose has a bridge that is high and noticeable. A pug nose is short and wide. It usually turns up at the end.

Predictions Chart

When you read a story, you often make **predictions** about what might happen next. Writers often plant clues on purpose. The clues suggest in advance, or **foreshadow,** what will happen later. For this reason, the clues are sometimes called **foreshadowing.**

Now that you've read "After Twenty Years," go back and look for clues. Then, fill out the charts below with the clues and with the events that the clues foreshadow. One clue and the event it foreshadows has been filled in for you.

Foreshadowing Clues	What the Clues Foreshadow
Bob hides in the shadows.	Bob is a criminal.

What's *Really* in a Name?

Reading Skill: Perspective

Perspective is the way we look at a subject. It is our point of view toward something. Take school uniforms, for example. Some people don't like them. They think students should be allowed to dress the way they wish. Other people think school uniforms are a good idea. They think uniforms help do away with clothes competition. Who's right? Well, that is a matter of perspective.

All writers have a particular perspective on their subjects. You may have already read "After Twenty Years" by O. Henry. O. Henry's perspective in that story is clear. Life offers us choices between honest and dishonest behavior. O. Henry clearly favors honesty, even though friendship is at risk.

Into the Article

In this article, the author remembers a childhood friend. That friend became an actress. When she did this, she changed her name. Why would she do this? The author is troubled by the change. Then the author finds out there is more than one reason to choose a new name. She sees the situation from a different perspective. What do you think?

What's Really in a Name?

HELLO
my name is

Jack

Based on the Article by

Joan Burditt

1   Patsy seemed like a movie star before she became one. She was my sister's friend. She was only in the sixth grade, but she seemed almost grown up to seven-year-old me.

   As an adult, Patsy was on television and in movies. Once 5 I looked for her name in the credits. It wasn't there. Then my sister said Patsy had changed her name. She had a pseudonym, a made-up or fake name.

   I felt confused. Why did she need a new name?

   Writers may use fake names called pen names. William 10 Sydney Porter, the famous short story writer, called himself O. Henry. Mark Twain's name was really Samuel Clemens.

   Writers may use pen names to sell books. Porter had a criminal record. As an ex-convict, he might have had trouble getting his books published. So he changed his name.

15   Archibald Lynn Joscelyn writes westerns. He changed his name to Al Cody. (Think of Buffalo Bill Cody.) The romance writer Elaine Carr is really a man. His name is Charles Mason.

   Many people want names that are easy to remember. 20 Which has a better ring—Charles Lutwidge Dodgson or Lewis Carroll? Reginald Dwight or Elton John? Ralph Lifshitz or Ralph Lauren? Norma Jean Baker or Marilyn Monroe?

   Why am I troubled about Patsy's name change? I thought 25 Patsy changed her name to get rid of her past. Her old friends, the neighborhood, even me. Patsy, Norma Jean, Reginald—they probably all had good reasons for choosing new names. But I hope they held on to their roots. I agree with writer James Baldwin. He said, "Know from whence[1] 30 you came. If you know from whence you came, there are absolutely no limitations to where you can go."

---

1. whence: where.

Perspective Chart

After you finish reading "What's *Really* in a Name?" fill out the chart below. It should help you identify the writer's perspective on changing names. Part of the chart has been done for you.

The writer doesn't understand why Patsy changed her name.

↓

Why do some people change their names? **1.** Writers use pen names to sell books. **2.** **3.**

↓

What is the writer's main concern about changing names?

↓

What is the final quotation in the article?

↓

What is the writer's perspective on changing names?

Bargain

Literary Focus: Point of View

A story's **point of view** depends on who is telling the story. "Bargain" is told by Al, a character in the story. A story that is told by a character in the story is told from a **first-person point of view.** We see the story the way that character sees it. We know what that character thinks and feels. Stories told from a first-person point of view are easy to recognize because the narrator often uses the pronoun *I*.

Reading Skill: Making Predictions

As you read this story, try to guess what will happen next. This process of guessing is called **making predictions.** Here's how to make predictions:

Look for clues in the story.	Draw on your own experience and knowledge.

Make your prediction.

If you guess right, you can congratulate yourself. If you guess wrong, you can enjoy the surprise of what really happens.

Into the Story

This story takes place in the Old West, before cars and airplanes were invented. Towns were far apart, and people used wagons and horses to travel between them. The town in the story is so far from where the train stops that it takes two days to get there. There are no hotels along the road. Travelers have to sleep outside, even in bad weather.

BARGAIN

Based on the Story by
A. B. Guthrie

Here's HOW

POINT OF VIEW

In lines 1–2, I can see that the story is in the first-person point of view. The narrator uses the pronoun *I*.

Here's HOW

MAKING PREDICTIONS

I bet there's going to be more trouble between Mr. Baumer and Slade. They're such different characters! Mr. Baumer works hard to build his business. Slade is rude and doesn't pay his bills. I wonder if Mr. Baumer will get hurt.

Your TURN

POINT OF VIEW

We find out about Mr. Baumer through the details Al tells us. Underline the words Al uses to tell about Mr. Baumer in lines 19–28.

1   **M**r. Baumer and I had closed his store and were walking to the post office to mail the bills. We saw Freighter Slade standing alone in front of the saloon. Mr. Baumer held out a bill to Slade.

5   "What do you want, Dutchie?" Slade said.

"Twenty-one dollars and fifty cents—for the things you bought."

"You know what I do with bills, Dutchie?" Slade crumpled the envelope and dropped it. Then he took Mr.

10 Baumer's nose between two fingers and twisted it hard. He turned and went into the bar.

Mr. Baumer picked up the bill and smoothed it. He didn't say anything, and I felt embarrassed for him. After he mailed the bills, we walked home together.

15   "Study, Al," he told me. "It's important to know how to read and write and do math."

I'd been working for Mr. Baumer in the summer and after school since my dad died.

The store wasn't big, but it had groceries on one side

20 and clothing and cloth on the other. In the back were kerosene,[1] whiskey, buckets, and tools. It would have closed long ago if Mr. Baumer hadn't been so stubborn and worked so hard.

The next afternoon, Mr. Baumer was sitting at his desk.

25 He was a small, bent man with a little belly. The only thing unusual about him was his chin, which looked like a little pink hill. Carefully he touched his nose. When he saw me, he sighed, "That Slade."

"It's useless sending him a bill, Mr. Baumer. He can't even

30 read, and he doesn't pay anybody."

---

1. **kerosene** (kehr uh SEEN): a thin, petroleum-based oil used as fuel.

"Bargain" adapted from *The Big It and Other Stories* by A. B. Guthrie. Copyright © 1960 by A. B. Guthrie. Retold by Holt, Rinehart and Winston. All rights reserved. Reproduced by permission of **Houghton Mifflin Company.**

"I think he hates me for coming from another country. I came here at sixteen, I learned to read and write, and now I own a business."

"He hates everybody."

35 "But he doesn't pinch everybody's nose—or call them Dutchie."

"You shouldn't have sold Slade anything unless he paid first."

"I know," he answered. "A man makes mistakes."

40 "I think you'd better forget Slade's bill."

"But it's not about money anymore, Al."

"Then, what is it?"

He thought a little. "It is the thing. You see, it's the thing."

45 I didn't know what he meant. "Slade steals whiskey and other things from the merchandise he carries," he continued.

"All the freighters steal whiskey," I told him. The fifty-mile trip from the train took at least two days with one overnight

50 stop. Freighters would drill a hole in a whiskey barrel and take some. Then they'd say that the missing whiskey had evaporated.

"Even Moore, who carries your freight, steals whiskey."

"Yes," Mr. Baumer said. I watched his eyes—thinking.

55 For a month nothing happened. Early in October, Mr. Baumer and I were walking to the post office with his bills. It was dark, and I didn't see Slade right away. He was standing in front of the bar just like last time.

When he saw Slade, Mr. Baumer asked me to find

60 Slade's bill. The next thing I knew, Mr. Baumer was falling, dropping the envelopes. Slade had hit him hard on his back, saying, "How're you, Dutchie?" Meanwhile, Dr. King and another man had come along and were watching.

Here's HOW

POINT OF VIEW

I've underlined a key sentence in line 45. It shows that a first-person point of view is limited. Al thinks Mr. Baumer is angry with Slade because of the money. However, Mr. Baumer says that it's not about the money anymore. It's the "thing," the principle. His anger runs deep.

Here's HOW

VOCABULARY

I see the word *freighters* in line 48. The dictionary says that a freighter is someone who gets paid for moving merchandise or goods from one place to another. Some of these goods will be sold in Mr. Baumer's store.

Your TURN

MAKING PREDICTIONS

Based on what you've learned about the characters, what do you think will happen next?

_____

_____

_____

Here's
HOW

POINT OF VIEW

In lines 72–77, I know how Al
feels about what happened
to Mr. Baumer because the
story is in the first-person
point of view. I know that
Al thinks Slade should be
punished. What I do not know
is what Mr. Baumer thinks.

Your
TURN

POINT OF VIEW

In lines 78–85, we find out
that Mr. Baumer has again
hired Slade. Because the
story is told from the first-
person point of view, we
know only what Al is
thinking. What important
information is missing
because Al doesn't know it?

_____

_____

_____

_____

_____

_____

Then Slade slugged Mr. Baumer, knocking him flat.

65 Before he could get up, Slade crushed Mr. Baumer's right hand with his boot heel.

Dr. King saw what had happened. He looked Mr. Baumer over and said to Slade, "I think you've broken his hand."

70 "He's lucky I didn't kill him," said Slade. "If you don't stay away from me, Dutchie, I'll give you more of the same!"

The next day Mr. Baumer's hand was in a sling, and he couldn't work much. I told him I would get the law after Slade, but he said the law wasn't good at settling plain

75 fights.

"Well, I'd do something."

"Yes, you would, Al."

Six weeks before Christmas, Mr. Baumer hired Slade to carry his freight. I could hardly believe it. Ed Hempel, the

80 new clerk, told me that Mr. Baumer had sent him to find Slade and that he'd seen them talking in the store. Then Mr. Baumer told Moore he'd changed to Slade.

Mr. Baumer never said anything to me about hiring Slade. I felt really bad because I couldn't look up to him

85 anymore, even though I wanted to.

Slade brought in several loads for Mr. Baumer. Before Christmas the weather turned very cold. One afternoon it was 42 degrees below zero.

That day Moore came into the store to tell us Slade was

90 dead. "I guess your new man froze to death."

"He knows too much to freeze," Mr. Baumer said.

"He's sure frozen now. He's in the wagon outside. I found him doubled up in the snow with no fire. I had an extra man, so I brought your load in. But your stuff will have

95 to wait."

I went to look at Slade. His body was bent, as if he had frozen leaning forward in a chair.

Mr. Connor, the undertaker, took Slade's body away.

It was beginning to get dark, so Mr. Baumer told Colly, 100 Ed, and me to unload the wagon. One of the last things we unloaded was a barrel.

"Mr. Baumer, we'll never sell all this, will we?"

"Sure we will, Al. I got it cheap—a bargain."

I looked at the barrel again. In big letters were the 105 words "Wood Alcohol—Deadly Poison."

"Hurry. It's late." For a second I saw a hard look in his eyes. I saw, you might say, that hilly chin reflected in his eyes. "Then we go home, Al. It's good to know how to read."

MAKING PREDICTIONS

Well, I predicted that Mr. Baumer would eventually win this fight. But I didn't think Mr. Baumer would go that far! Mr. Baumer expected freighters like Slade to drink from the whiskey barrels they carried. He hired Slade because he wanted Slade to drink the poison.

Your TURN

MAKING PREDICTIONS

Good writers often have you guessing what will happen next even when the story is over. Do you think Mr. Baumer will get caught? Why or why not?

_____

_____

_____

_____

_____

_____

First-Person Point of View

A story that is told by a character in the story is told from a **first-person point of view.** We know what that character thinks and feels. However, we don't always know what the *other* characters think and feel.

Analyzing Point of View

The story "Bargain" is told from Al's point of view. The story surprises us because we don't always know what the other characters are thinking. Now that you've read the story, answer the questions below. Part of the chart has been completed for you.

A. What do we know about Al?

1. He works for Mr. Baumer.

2. _____

B. What does Al tell us about Mr. Baumer?

1. _____

2. Mr. Baumer thinks it's important to know how to read and write.

C. What does Al tell us about Slade?

1. _____

2. He steals whiskey from freight trains.

D. What important information does Al __NOT__ know?

_____

_____

_____

_____

Vocabulary

Some words have more than one meaning. In "Bargain," the word *envelope* refers to a folded paper container for a letter. *Envelope* can also refer to the safe operating limits of something, such as an airplane. An airplane flying outside its envelope would be flying dangerously. When you come across a **multiple-meaning word,** you can use the surrounding words, phrases, and sentences to figure out its meaning.

Use a dictionary to write two possible meanings for each of these words from "Bargain." The first one has been done for you.

	Meaning in Story	**Other Meaning**
bill (line 4)	A request for money due	A bird's beak
drill (line 50)		
knocking (line 64)		
sling (line 72)		

Yeh-Shen

Literary Focus: Omniscient Point of View

Who can watch all the characters in a story even when they're sleeping? Who can understand each character's most secret thoughts? Who knows what each character will do next?—an *omniscient*, or all-knowing, narrator, of course! A narrator who tells a story from the **omniscient point of view** knows everything about the characters. This omniscient narrator is *not* a character in the story. This narrator sees everything, but the characters can't see this narrator.

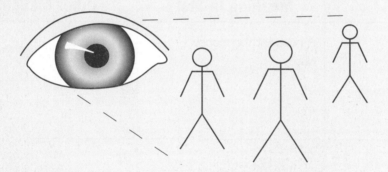

Reading Skill: Making Connections

"What does this story have to do with me?" You might ask that question when you're reading a new story. Relating new stories to your own world or to stories you already know can help you understand the new story better. **Making connections** can also give you insight into your own life.

Into the Folk Tale

Did you know that the first Cinderella story comes from China and is over one thousand years old? There are more than nine hundred versions of "Cinderella." The version you probably know best was collected in 1697 by a French writer named Charles Perrault. "Yeh-Shen" is the Chinese version.

Yeh-Shen

BASED ON THE FOLK TALE RETOLD BY
Ai-Ling Louie

Here's
HOW

**MAKING
CONNECTIONS**

Two wives? I don't remember
that Cinderella's father has
two wives! In the version I
know, Cinderella's mother
dies, and then her father
marries again. Hmm. I also
don't remember anything
about Cinderella becoming
friends with a fish. However,
the relationship between Yeh-
Shen and her stepmother is
very familiar.

Here's
HOW

**OMNISCIENT POINT
OF VIEW**

This narrator seems to
know everything about all the
characters. In line 6, for
example, the narrator says
that Yeh-Shen's stepmother
is jealous. That's why she
gives Yeh-Shen the hardest
work. The narrator also
knows the secrets that Yeh-
Shen keeps from her
stepmother. I wonder what
the story would be like if it
were told from the
stepmother's point of view.

1 Long ago, a chief named Wu lived in a cave in China with his two wives. Each of them had a baby daughter. But then Chief Wu and one of his wives got sick and died.

The little orphan daughter, named Yeh-Shen, grew up in
5 her stepmother's home. Yeh-Shen was as bright and lovely as her stepsister was plain. Her stepmother was jealous of Yeh-Shen and gave her the hardest work to do.

Yeh-Shen's only friend was a golden-eyed fish. She shared the little food she had with the fish, and it grew large.

10 When the stepmother heard of this friendship, she was very angry that Yeh-Shen had kept a secret from her. She went down to the pond and lured the fish to the bank. There she killed it and took it home to cook for dinner.

When Yeh-Shen found her pet was gone, she fell to the
15 ground and cried into the pond.

"Ah, poor child!" a voice said.

An old man in ragged clothes was looking down at her. He told her that her stepmother had killed the fish. Yeh-Shen gasped. The old man went on. "I have come to bring you a
20 gift. Listen. The bones of your fish are filled with a powerful spirit. Whenever you really need something, kneel before the bones. Let them know your heart's desire. But do not waste their gifts."

With that, the old man rose into the sky. Yeh-Shen sadly
25 went to the trash to get her friend's bones.

Yeh-Shen was often left alone after that. The sad girl took comfort in speaking to the bones of her fish. She was often hungry, and she would ask the bones for food.

Adaptation of *Yeh-Shen: A Cinderella Story from China*, retold by Ai-Ling Louie.
Text copyright © 1982 by Ai-Ling Louie. All rights reserved. Retold by Holt, Rinehart
and Winston. Reproduced by permission of **Philomel Books, an imprint of
Penguin Putnam Books for Young Readers, a Member of Penguin Group (USA)
Inc., 345 Hudson St., New York, NY 10014.** Electronic format by permission of
McIntosh and Otis, Inc.

The spring festival time came near, when young men and
30 women hoped to meet the person they would marry. Yeh-
Shen longed to go. However, her stepmother wanted to find a
husband for her own daughter first.

On the holiday the stepmother and her daughter dressed
in their best clothes and set out for the festival. They made
35 Yeh-Shen stay home to guard the fruit trees.

As soon as she was alone, Yeh-Shen went to kneel before
the bones of her fish. "Oh, dear friend," she said, "I long to
go to the festival, but I have no nice clothes."

At once, she found herself dressed in a sky-blue dress and
40 a feathered cloak. On her feet were golden slippers. When
she walked in them, her feet were as light as air.

"Be sure not to lose the golden shoes," said the spirit of
the bones. Yeh-Shen promised to be careful and went off to
join the festival.

45 All day at the festival, people around Yeh-Shen whispered,
"Look at that beautiful girl! Who is she?"

Then she heard her stepsister: "Mother, she looks like
Yeh-Shen!"

Yeh-Shen quickly ran off. As she ran she lost one of her
50 golden slippers. When it fell off, her fine clothes turned back
to rags. Only one thing remained—a tiny golden shoe.

Yeh-Shen ran to the bones of her fish and returned the
slipper. The bones were silent. Yeh-Shen realized she'd lost
her only friend. She hid the little shoe in her bed and went
55 outside, where she cried until she fell asleep with her arms
around a fruit tree.

Meanwhile, a villager found the shoe and sold it to a
merchant. The merchant gave it to the king of T'o Han. The
king marveled at the tiny slipper's beauty. He decided to find
60 the woman who owned it.

Your TURN

MAKING CONNECTIONS

People around the world have been telling the Cinderella story for ages. Do you recognize features on this page that appear in another version of "Cinderella"? If so, list two of them below.

1. _____
   _____

2. _____

Why do you think the Cinderella story is so popular? What deep human wishes and fears does it express?

_____
_____
_____

Here's HOW

VOCABULARY

At first, I wasn't sure what *marveled* (line 58) meant. Then, I realized that this word is similar to the word *marvelous*. I bet line 58 means that the king thought the slipper was marvelous, or wonderful.

Here's HOW

MAKING CONNECTIONS

In line 68, the king is impressed by Yeh-Shen's tiny feet. I can make a connection between Yeh-Shen's beauty and what I learned in another class about foot binding in Chinese culture. In the old days, many Chinese women wrapped their feet so tightly that their feet became tiny. They did this to be pretty. These women had twisted, broken feet, and they could barely walk. (This practice now is against the law in China.)

Your TURN

OMNISCIENT POINT OF VIEW

Check back to what the narrator told you about Yeh-Shen's stepmother. How would the story change if the stepmother, instead of the omniscient narrator, were telling it?

_____

_____

_____

_____

_____

All the women from the area were called to try on the shoe, but no one claimed it. Under cover of darkness, Yeh-Shen finally dared to come. She tiptoed across the floor of the building containing the shoe and looked carefully.
65 Recognizing it, she took it to return to the fish bones, so her friend would speak to her again.

The king was about to have Yeh-Shen arrested. Then he noticed her lovely face shining from her ragged clothes. He also saw she had the tiniest feet he had ever seen.

70 The king waved to his men. The girl in rags was allowed to leave with the golden slipper. Quietly, the king's men followed her home.

Yeh-Shen was about to hide both shoes in her bed when there was a pounding on the door. Yeh-Shen found the king
75 at her door. He spoke to her kindly and asked her to try on the shoes. As soon as she put them on, her rags once more became the feathered cloak and beautiful sky-blue gown.

The king knew he'd found his true love.

Not long after this, Yeh-Shen was married to the king. The
80 king would not allow her to bring her wicked stepmother and stepsister to his palace. And one day, it is said, both were crushed to death in a shower of flying stones.

Making Connections: Brainstorm

"This story is outdated. Girls don't sit around and wait to be rescued any longer." Maybe that's what you thought when you read this story. Well, now is your turn to update the Cinderella story! Think about how you could retell the Cinderella story by **making connections** to your world.

To brainstorm how you would rewrite the Cinderella story, answer the questions below.

1. In the folk tale you just read, Yeh-Shen is an underdog, a person who seems to be marked as a loser. In your story, who would be the underdog?

_____

_____

_____

_____

2. Who or what would hold the underdog back?

_____

_____

_____

_____

3. How would the underdog get out of the bad situation?

_____

_____

_____

_____

Names/Nombres

Reading Skill: Main Idea and Details

The **main idea** is the point of a piece of writing. If you are asked to say in a few words what an article is about, you are being asked for the main idea. A selection has an overall main idea. A paragraph within a selection may also have a main idea. Sometimes, the writer will state the main idea. Other times, a writer will give you clues and let you figure out the main idea for yourself. When a main idea is hinted at but not directly stated, it is called an **implied main idea.**

A good writer will give you clues to figure out the main idea. Your job is to find those important **details** and fit them together like a puzzle. Once all the pieces are together, the main idea should be clear. You may want to use an organizer like the one below to record your information.

Details	Main Idea

Into the Essay

You've probably noticed that people from different places may pronounce things in different ways. Usually, we can understand what people are saying. But what about names? Does it bother you if someone doesn't say your name the way you do? This story is about a girl who has a name that many people pronounce the wrong way.

Names/Nombres

Based on the Essay by

Julia
Alvarez

Here's
HOW

VOCABULARY

I see the word *immigration* in line 2. I think it means "when people come into a new country to live" because the story begins "When we came to New York City, . . ."

Here's
HOW

MAIN IDEA

I think I see the main idea in the first paragraph. The writer is upset when people pronounce her name the wrong way. She doesn't tell us this directly, but we know that's how she feels. She wants to correct the immigration officer, but she's afraid he will keep her out of the country.

Your
TURN

DETAILS

Lines 11–16 give details about the different ways people say the names of the writer and her family. If you put all these details together, what is the main idea for the paragraph?

_____

_____

_____

1 **W**hen we came to New York City, our names changed right away. The immigration officer asked my father, *Mister Elbures*, if he had anything to declare. My father shook his head no. We were waved through. I was afraid of being
5 turned away if I corrected the man's pronunciation. But I said our name to myself. I opened my mouth wide for the blast of the *a*. I trilled[1] my tongue for the *r, All-vah-rrr-es!*

At the hotel, my mother was *Missus Alburest*. I was *little girl,* as in, "Hey, little girl, stop riding the elevator up and
10 down. It's *not* a toy."

We moved into our new apartment building. The manager there called my father *Mister Alberase.* The neighbors who became mother's friends called her *Jew-lee-ah* instead *of Hoo-lee-ah.* I was known as *Hoo-lee-tah* at home.
15 But at school I was *Judy* or *Judith.* Once an English teacher called me *Juliet.*

Getting used to my new names took a while. I wanted to correct my teachers and new friends. But my mother said it didn't matter. "You know what your friend Shakespeare
20 said, 'A rose by any other name would smell as sweet.'"[2] Because I wrote stories and poems, my family called any famous author "my friend."

By high school, I was a popular kid. My friends called me *Jules* or *Hey Jude.* One group of friends called me *Alcatraz.*
25 My "Wanted" poster would read *JUDY ALCATRAZ.* Who would ever trace[3] her to me?

My older sister, *Mauricia,* had the hardest time. She and I were the family's Americans. We had been born in

---

1. **trilled:** made a rapid, vibrating sound.
2. *"A rose . . . as sweet":* Julia's mother is quoting from the play *Romeo and Juliet.*
3. **trace:** to follow the path of someone or something.

New York City. Then our parents had gotten homesick and
30 gone "home." My mother told of how she had almost
changed my sister's name.

Some of the new mothers were talking about their
babies' names. Among the Sallys and Johns, my mother
was shy about her baby's rich, noisy name. She gave her
35 baby's name as *Maureen.*

"Why did you give her an Irish name?" one woman
asked. "There are so many pretty Spanish names."

My mother blushed. She said her mother-in-law had
just died. Her husband wanted to call the first daughter for
40 his mother, *Mauran.* My mother thought the name was ugly.
She added part of her own mother's name, *Felicia,* to
Mauran.

"Her name is *Mao-ree-shee-ah,*" my mother told the
women.

45 "Why, that's a beautiful name," the new mothers cried.
"Moor-ee-sha," they said. *Moor-ee-sha* it was when we
returned to the States eleven years later. Sometimes she was
called *Maria* or *Marsha* by mistake.

My little sister, Ana, had the easiest time of all. She was
50 plain *Anne.* She turned out to be the family's pale, blond
"American beauty." Her boyfriends sometimes called her
Anita or *Anita Banana.*

By her college years in the late sixties, using names from
other countries was popular. Once a roommate answered
55 when I called Ana.

"Can I speak to Ana?" I asked, saying her name the
American way.

"Ana? Oh, you must mean *Ah-nah!*"

As time passed, I no longer cared about my name
60 being pronounced right. I just wanted to be Judy. I wanted
to fit in with the Sallys and Janes in my class. But my

Here's
HOW

VOCABULARY

The word *homesick* in line
29 is new to me, but I think I
know the answer because
homesick is made up of two
little words—*home* and *sick.*
The writer's parents missed
home so much, they felt sick.

Here's
HOW

MAIN IDEA

In lines 38–42, I see that the
writer's mother wants to
honor her mother-in-law, but
she doesn't want to give her
baby an ugly name. So, she
makes up a name by adding
part of her own mother's
name. That's pretty clever.

Your
TURN

MAIN IDEA

The details in lines 43–46
show the writer's mother
telling people how to say
her daughter's name, and
how the people say it the
wrong way. What is the
implied main idea in these
lines?

_____

_____

_____

Here's HOW

DETAILS

In lines 75-78, the writer includes several details that show that she sometimes likes being different. When her friends ask her to say her name in Spanish, she enjoys making "mouths drop." She also tells her friends all twelve of her names. If she wasn't proud of being different, she wouldn't have told them all twelve names.

Your TURN

DETAILS

The main idea in lines 79–83 is that the writer's family is different in several ways, not just in how they say their names. Circle details the writer gives in this paragraph to lead us to this main idea.

accent and looks gave me away. People would say, "So where are you from, Judy?"

"New York," I said. After all, I had been born blocks

65 away.

"I mean, *originally.*"

"From the Caribbean," I answered.

"Really? I've been to Bermuda. We went last April. I got the worst sunburn! So, are you from Portoriko?"[4]

70 "No," I sighed. "From the Dominican Republic."

"Where's that?"

"South of Bermuda."

I knew they didn't mean to hurt me. Still, I did not like being seen as different.

75 "Say your name in Spanish, oh, please say it!" I made mouths drop one day by saying my twelve names: "Julia Altagracia María Teresa Álvarez Tavares Perello Espaillat Julia Pérez Rochet González."

My different background was really clear when my

80 whole family attended school events. Aunts, uncles, and the many little cousins came to my graduation. They sat in the first row to try to understand the fast American speakers. But then they spoke loudly among themselves.

Introducing them to my friends was hard. These

85 relatives had long names. There were so many of them. Their connections to me were hard to understand. There was my aunt Tía[5] Josefina, who was really a much older cousin. One uncle Tío José brought my godmother, Tía Amelia. My friends usually had only "Mom and Dad" to

90 introduce.

After the graduation, my family waited outside. My

---

4. **Portoriko:** This spelling makes fun of the schoolmates' pronunciation of Puerto Rico.
5. **Tía** (TEE uh): Spanish for "Aunt." **Tío** is "Uncle."

friends and I signed yearbooks with nicknames like "Beans" and "Pepperoni" and "Alcatraz." We hugged and cried. We promised to keep in touch.

95 　 Our goodbyes went on too long. I heard my father's voice calling, *"Hoo-lee-tah!"*

Back home, my large family gave me a party. The cake said *Happy Graduation, Julie.* There were many gifts. My parents gave me the biggest gift—a typewriter for writing my
100 stories and poems.

The family said that someday my name would be well known. I laughed, wondering which one I would go by.

Your
TURN

DETAILS

Do you think that Julia's parents are happy that she might become a writer? In lines 97–100, find and underline the detail that backs up your answer.

_____

Main Idea and Details Map

Fill in the following map with details from "Names/Nombres." (One detail has already been added to the map.) Then, review those details and decide what the main idea is.

Write the main idea in the center of the map.

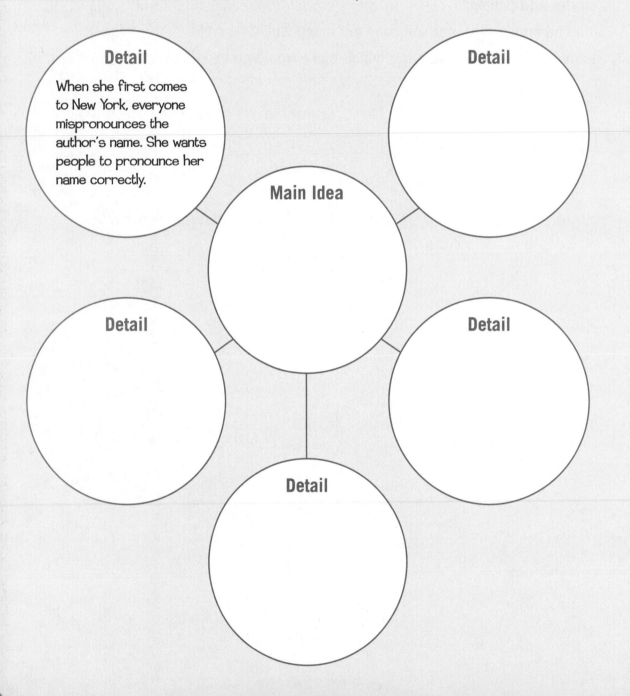

Detail

When she first comes to New York, everyone mispronounces the author's name. She wants people to pronounce her name correctly.

Detail

Main Idea

Detail

Detail

Detail

Vocabulary

A. Match each vocabulary word with its definition. Write the letter of the correct definition on the line next to the word. One word has already been done for you.

_____ **1.** immigration

a. the government office that allows people from other countries to enter the United States

___b___ **2.** trill

b. a rapid, vibrating sound made in pronouncing certain letters of a language

_____ **3.** trace

c. to follow the path of someone or something

_____ **4.** homesick

d. missing home and family while away from them

B. Choose two words from the list above. Use each word in a sentence.

1. _____

_____

_____

_____

2. _____

_____

_____

_____

Amigo Brothers

Literary Focus: Conflict

Conflict is the problem or struggle that makes a story interesting. In "Amigo Brothers," there are two kinds of conflict: external and internal. The boxing match is an **external conflict.** The **internal conflicts** are in the characters' minds—How can they fight one another and remain friends?

Reading Skill: Comparison and Contrast

Comparing and contrasting help you see and analyze details more clearly. When you **compare,** you point out what is the same. When you **contrast,** you point out what is different. To compare and contrast the two boys in "Amigo Brothers," put the information in a diagram such as this one.

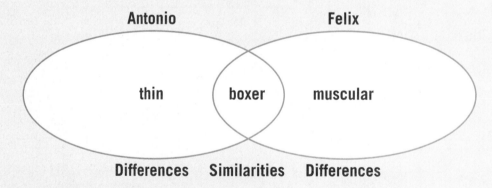

Antonio		**Felix**
thin	boxer	muscular
Differences	**Similarities**	**Differences**

Into the Story

This story is about two friends **(amigos)** in New York City. There, each dreams of becoming a boxing champion. Then, they find out they have to fight each other. The winner will represent their club in a big tournament. The fight gets closer. Both friends want to win, but neither wants to hurt his best friend. The story compares and contrasts the ways the friends handle the conflicts in their minds before the fight.

Amigo Brothers

Based on the Story by
Piri Thomas

Behind the Story

Many boys from the Lower East Side of New York City have dreamed of building a better life for themselves. Some have tried by entering the New York Golden Gloves boxing tournament. This tournament was started in 1927 by Paul Gallico, a newspaper writer. This tournament marks an amateur's entry into the world of big-time boxing.

Here's HOW

COMPARISON AND CONTRAST

This story is all about similarities and differences. I'll start with the two characters, Antonio and Felix. The guys are the same age, live in the same place, and have the same dream. But they don't look alike, and they don't fight alike. Maybe I should put these facts in a diagram.

Your TURN

COMPARISON AND CONTRAST

In lines 18–24, the two friends talk about the fight. On the line below, write whether their feelings about the fight are the same or different.

_____

Your TURN

VOCABULARY

Pulling can mean "drawing something toward you," "moving," "carrying out with skill," "attracting," or "tearing." Which meaning do you think it has in line 20?

_____

1 **A**ntonio Cruz and Felix Vargas were both seventeen. They had been best friends for so long they felt like brothers. They lived in the same apartment house on the Lower East Side of Manhattan. Antonio was light-skinned, tall, and
5 thin. Felix was dark, short, and muscular.

Both dreamed of becoming the world lightweight boxing champion. They trained together. Early mornings, they ran along the river together.

Both had won four boxing medals. Their styles were
10 different, though. Antonio had a longer reach and was a better boxer, but Felix was a more powerful slugger.

In just two weeks, they would fight each other. The winner would represent their club in the Golden Gloves Championship Tournament.

15 As they ran one morning, Felix said they needed to stop and talk. Their match was less than a week away. They leaned against the railing, looking out at the river.

"I don't know how to say this, bro," Felix began.

"I've been worrying about our fight, too, panin.[1] I don't
20 sleep. I think about pulling punches so I don't hurt you."

"Me, too," said Felix. "I want to win fair and square. Let's make a promise, OK? When we fight, we've gotta be like strangers."

"Sí,"[2] Antonio agreed.

25 "Listen, Tony, I think we shouldn't see each other until the fight. I'm going to Aunt Lucy's in the Bronx. I'll train up there."

---

1. panin (pah NEEN): Puerto Rican Spanish slang for "pal" or "buddy."
2. sí: Spanish for "yes."

"Amigo Brothers" adapted from *Stories from El Barrio* by Piri Thomas. Copyright © 1978 by **Piri Thomas.** Retold by Holt, Rinehart and Winston. Reproduced by permission of the author.

Felix suggested they split right there. After the fight, he said, they'd be together again like nothing ever

30 happened. They hugged and went their separate ways.

The night before the fight, Antonio went up to the roof. The only way not to hurt Felix, he thought, was to knock him out quickly. He worried about what the fight would do to their friendship.

35 That night, Felix watched a boxing movie, imagining himself as the hero. It was Felix the Champion against Antonio the Challenger. He hoped for a quick, clean knockout, too.

On the day of the tournament, fans filled Tompkins

40 Square Park. In their dressing rooms, Antonio put on white trunks, black socks, and black shoes. Felix wore light blue trunks, red socks, and white shoes.

There were six matches before their fight. Finally, it was time. The crowd roared as they entered the ring.

45 *Bong! Bong! Bong!* "Ladies and Gentlemen, Señores[3] and Señoras.[4] For the main event we have two young Puerto Rican boxers. Felix Vargas at 134 pounds and Antonio Cruz at 133 pounds."

The referee told them to fight cleanly. "Now shake hands

50 and come out fighting."

The bell sounded for round one. Felix punched a hard straight left, but Antonio slipped away. Antonio's three fast lefts snapped Felix's head back. Felix knew then that Antonio wasn't pulling any punches. Both would fight to win.

55 Antonio danced around, punching again and again. Felix moved in closer so he could reach Antonio. At the end of the round, he trapped Antonio against the ropes

Here's HOW

CONFLICT

This story is about conflicts. There's the fight I can see. That's an external conflict. Then, there are the fights I can't see—the internal conflicts. Those are inside Felix's and Antonio's heads. Both guys want to win, but not by hurting their friend or the friendship. Wow! Talk about a no-win situation!

Your TURN

VOCABULARY

The word *trunks* can mean "large chests," "enclosed auto compartments," "stems of trees," "elephants' noses," or "very short trousers." What meaning do you think it has in line 41?

_____

_____

Your TURN

CONFLICT

The beginning of the fight is described in lines 51–54. Underline the sentence that tells you both boys have solved the conflicts in their heads.

Here's HOW

COMPARISON AND CONTRAST

Here are some more comparisons. Both Felix and Antonio are injured, but they are injured in different ways.

Your TURN

VOCABULARY

The word *batter* has several meanings. It can mean "cake dough," "a player at bat in baseball," or "to hit or strike with repeated blows." What meaning do you think the word *batter* has in line 77?

_____

_____

_____

_____

and smashed his abdomen. Two hard lefts to his head set Felix's ear ringing.

60   *Bong!* Both boxers froze mid-punch as round one ended.

Felix's right ear rang as he moved to his corner. Antonio had red marks on his midribs. "Remember," Antonio's trainer told him, "Felix always goes for the body."

65   Felix's trainer warned him, too. "You gotta get in close, or he'll chop you up from way back."

Bong! Bong! Round two. Felix rushed in and landed a solid right to the head. Hurt, Antonio hit back hard and fast. Felix returned a left to Antonio's head and a right to the

70   body.

Antonio waited while Felix danced around. Then, Felix rushed in and slugged Antonio. Antonio hit him hard on the chin, and lights exploded inside Felix's head. His legs folded, but he managed to fight off Antonio's attack. Felix came back

75   with a powerful right.

Antonio smashed Felix's right eye, which puffed up right away. Toe to toe, the boxers battered each other. Right, left, right, left. The crowd stood and roared.

A sudden right to the chin turned Antonio's legs to

80   jelly. Felix hit wildly until Antonio punched him hard on the nose.

Then Felix landed a fierce blow. Antonio dropped, then staggered to his feet. He slugged Felix hard, and Felix went down flat on his back.

85   He got up in a fog. The crowd roared wildly as the bell sounded the end of round two.

Both fighters were hurting, but the doctor said they were OK to continue.

Bong!—the last round. So far the fight seemed even, but

90   there could be no tie. There had to be a winner.

Antonio charged, driving Felix against the ropes. They pounded each other fiercely. Felix's eye was closed, and blood poured from Antonio's nose. The crowd watched in silence.

95 The bell sounded the end of the fight. But the boxers kept on pounding each other. The referee and trainers pulled them apart, and someone poured cold water over them.

Felix and Antonio looked around and hurried toward 100 each other. The audience cried out in alarm. Would they fight to the death? Then they cheered as the amigo brothers hugged.

"Ladies and Gentlemen, Señores and Señoras. The winner and champion is . . . " The announcer turned to point 105 to the winner.

But he stood alone in the ring. The champions had already left, arm in arm.

Comparison and Contrast

Finding Similarities and Differences

Piri Thomas begins his story by contrasting the two best friends. A **comparison** points out similarities between things. A **contrast** points out differences. Go back over the story. Use a Venn diagram like the one below to help you identify the ways in which Felix and Antonio are alike and different. Write their likenesses in the part where the circles overlap.

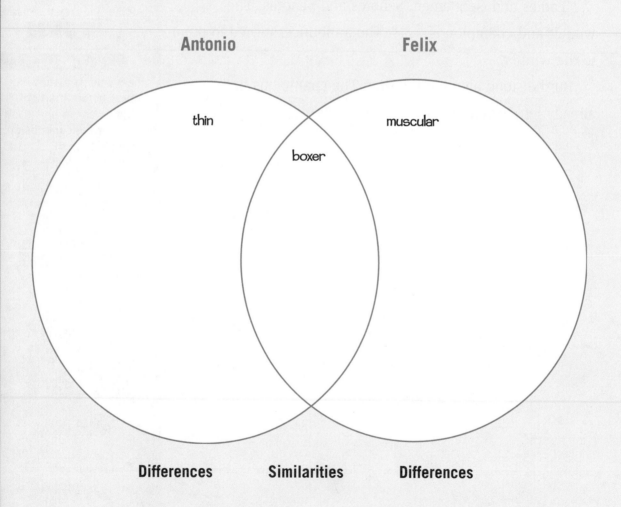

Antonio   Felix

thin   boxer   muscular

Differences   **Similarities**   **Differences**

Vocabulary and Comprehension

Use a dictionary or a thesaurus to find a **synonym** for each vocabulary word below. Next, write a sentence using each vocabulary word. Use context clues to make the meaning of the vocabulary word clear.

EXAMPLE: muscular: <u>strong</u>   <u>The weight lifter's arms are very muscular.</u>

Words	Synonyms	Sentences
1. abdomen (line 58):		
2. battered (line 77):		
3. froze (line 60):		
4. represent (line 13):		
5. staggered (line 83):		

from Barrio Boy

Literary Focus: Autobiography

If someone else is writing your life story, that person is
writing a **biography.** If you are writing your own life story, you
are writing an **autobiography.**

Reading Skill: Fact and Opinion

"Did this *really* happen?" "Is it true?" If you ask such
questions when you're reading, you're interested in facts. A
fact is a statement that can be proved true. *Sacramento is in
California* is a fact.

"What does the author think of this?" If you ask this
question, you're looking for an opinion. An **opinion** is a
personal feeling or belief that can't be proved true or false.
Sacramento is the best place in the world is an opinion.

Don't be fooled. People may state an opinion as if it were
fact. When in doubt, ask yourself, "Can this be proved?"

Statements	Fact	Opinion
Mix blue paint and red paint, and you will get purple paint.	√	
Anna looked better with long hair.		√

Into the Autobiography

Ernesto Galarza was born in 1905 in a small village in
western Mexico. In 1910, the Mexican Revolution began,
and Ernesto and his family ran away from the violence.
Eventually, they settled in Sacramento, California. There
they lived in the *barrio,* or Spanish-speaking neighborhood.

Barrio Boy

BASED ON AN EXCERPT FROM THE AUTOBIOGRAPHY BY
Ernesto Galarza

1   **O**ne morning, my mother and I walked to Lincoln School. The school was half a block long. It was a new, three-story building, painted yellow. It had a shingled roof, different from the red tile roof of my school in Mazatlán. I saw other
5   differences. None of them made me feel better.

My mother and I walked together into the school. She held my hand.

We had carefully planned my first day at school. Mrs. Dodson had told us how to find it. We had walked past
10   it several times. Friends in the barrio explained that the head of the school was called a principal. They said the principal was a lady, not a man. They also said there was always someone at school who spoke Spanish.

We found Miss Nettie Hopley's office. There was a sign on
15   the door. It was in both Spanish and English. It said "Principal."

Miss Hopley was at a desk to one side. She sat in a chair with wheels.

She half turned in the chair. We didn't know what she
20   said to us next. She gave us a big smile. We said nothing. She said more words we did not understand, but she had a friendly voice and a sparkle in her eyes. She showed us to the table. I almost tiptoed. I made sure my mother was between me and this gringo[1] lady. In seconds, I had to decide if she
25   was a friend or a menace.[2] We sat down.

Then Miss Hopley stood up. She was very tall, with a shapely figure. She seemed like a giant. I decided I liked her.

---

1. **gringo** (GRIHNG goh): in Latin America, an insulting term for "foreigner."
2. **menace** (MEHN uhs): threat, danger.

Excerpt adapted from *Barrio Boy* by Ernesto Galarza. Copyright © 1971 by **University of Notre Dame Press.** Retold by Holt, Rinehart and Winston. Reproduced by permission of the publisher.

She walked to the office door and called a name. A boy of about ten entered. He sat down at the table. He was brown
30 like us. He was plump. His shiny black hair was combed straight back.

Miss Hopley sat down with us. She asked us questions. We answered. The boy translated. My name was Ernesto. My mother's name was Henriqueta. My birth certificate was in
35 San Blas. Here was my last report card from my school in Mazatlán. Miss Hopley wrote things in a book. My mother signed a card.

As long as my mother stayed, I felt safe. Once the questions were over, my mother left. Then, Miss Hopley took
40 my hand. She led me to Miss Ryan's first grade.

Miss Ryan took me to a seat at the front of the room. I shrank into my seat and watched her carefully. Because I was so small, she seemed very tall.

During the next few weeks, I became less afraid of Miss
45 Ryan. She would bend over my desk to help me with English words. She'd often make happy announcements to the whole class. "Ito can read a sentence," she'd say. And small Japanese Ito would slowly read aloud. "Come, Skipper, come. Come and run." The class would listen in wonder.

50 There were many other first-graders learning English. They too had moments of glory like Ito's. I had my own the day I could say *butterfly*. I had been saying "boo-ter-flee." "Children," said Miss Ryan. "Ernesto has learned how to say *butterfly*!" And I said the word just as Miss Ryan had. Soon I
55 could read a sentence. "Come butterfly, come fly with me."

First-graders who didn't know English got private lessons. Miss Ryan and I would read about sheep and a scared chicken. She'd help me say words like *pasture, bow-wow-wow, hay,* and *pretty.* To my Mexican ear, these words had
60 too many sounds and letters.

Your
TURN

FACT AND OPINION

Re-read lines 32–37. What makes these statements **facts** and not opinions?

_____

_____

_____

_____

Here's
HOW

AUTOBIOGRAPHY

I like the way the author tells his story. He's grown up now, but he wants us to understand how he felt as a small boy on his first day in a school in the United States. I circled one of the sentences that shows this perspective.

Here's
HOW

VOCABULARY

I didn't understand lines 58-59 at first. One of my classmates told me that "bow-wow-wow" is the English way to mimic a dog barking. In my native language, Japanese, we say "Wanwan." I wonder how Spanish-speakers imitate dogs barking.

Your TURN

FACT AND OPINION

Re-read line 67. What makes this statement an **opinion** and not a fact?

_____

_____

_____

_____

Your TURN

FACT AND OPINION

Re-read lines 75–89.

1. What are the author's opinions on being an American?

_____

_____

2. What does he think of education?

_____

_____

3. How does he feel about his Mexican heritage?

_____

_____

Miss Ryan would make me watch her lips. Then I'd close my eyes as she said words I found hard to read. It felt like together we were learning the secrets of English and grieving over the tale of Bo-Peep.[3]

65 I graduated with honors from the first grade. The main reason was that I had fallen in love with Miss Ryan. We all loved her. She was on our side.

Students from Lincoln were from many different races. They all came from the lower part of town. I had three 70 friends in the second grade. Kazushi was Japanese. Matti was a skinny Italian boy. And Manuel was a fat Portuguese. He'd never get into a fight. Instead, he'd force you to the ground and sit on you. There were students from all over the world, as well as from the United States.

75 Miss Hopley and her teachers never let us forget why we were at Lincoln. Foreigners were to become good Americans. American-born students were to accept the rest of us. Off the school grounds, we insulted each other as adults did. On the playground, we would be sent to the principal's office for 80 calling someone a wop, a chink, a dago, or a greaser. But our teachers helped us see that racial hatred was wrong.

At Lincoln, we became American, but we didn't have to give up our own culture. The teachers called us the names our parents did. No one was ever scolded for speaking his 85 first language on the playground. We told stories about our countries. Miss Hopley showed wonder over these stories. Her eyes would open wide until they popped slightly.

She said I should become a proud American. But she also made it clear that there was no shame in being Mexican.

---

3. Bo-Peep (BOH PEEP): A character from a nursery rhyme that begins, "Little Bo-Peep has lost her sheep."

Fact or Opinion?

Ernesto Galarza offers both **facts** and **opinions** in his autobiography. Look back at the selection to fill out this chart. In the first column, read the statement. In the second column, answer the question. If you think the statement can be proved true or false, check the Fact column. If you think the statement can**not** be proved true or false, check the Opinion column. If two of the last three columns are filled in, find a statement in the autobiography that fits and write it in the first column. Parts of the chart have been completed for you.

Statement	Can it be proved true or false?	Fact	Opinion
1. The school building was painted yellow.			
2. Miss Hopley stood up.	Yes.		
3.	No.		✓
4. Many other kids were learning English.			
5. English words had too many sounds and letters.			
6.	No.		✓

A Mason-Dixon Memory

Literary Focus: The Essay

An **essay** is a short piece of prose that discusses a single topic. An essay can be about anything from freedom to how you feel about your cat. Essays can be very structured and formal in tone, or they can be personal and even storylike. An essay's structure and tone will depend on its **purpose.** To figure out the purpose of an essay, ask yourself these questions: Does the writer want to inform you? persuade you? entertain you? or do something else?

Reading Skill: Text Structures (Flashbacks)

"At 6:00, a man walked into a store. At 6:10, he asked the salesperson for a glass of water. . . ." Many stories simply have one event following after another, just as events do in real life. Sometimes, however, writers play with time by using **flashbacks.** A **flashback** is a scene that breaks the normal time order of a story to show an event from the past.

| 6:00: An old man named Bill walks into a store. | → | 6:11: Bill sees a boy who reminds him of his brother who died. |

| **Flashback to 1925:** Bill, a ten-year-old boy, is playing golf with his older brother. |

Into the Essay

In some ways, this is an essay about discrimination. Discrimination is treating people differently because of their skin color, their sex, or their beliefs. In other ways, this is an essay about friendship and what friends do for each other.

A Mason-Dixon Memory

Memory

Based on the Essay by
Clifton Davis

Here's HOW

ESSAY

This essay is not formal. It's personal. The writer tells us about his own experience. It seems he's going to tell us a story.

Here's HOW

VOCABULARY

I think the words *putting* (PUH tihng) *green* in line 19 have something to do with golf. The speaker talks about being at a country club where his team was going to play. I checked in the dictionary, and I was right. A putting green is the area of grass around the cup or hole. The grass is cut very short.

Your TURN

FLASHBACK

In lines 28–29, the story is about to shift to a flashback. Draw a line under the word that tells us a flashback is coming.

1 **D**ondré Green glanced nervously around the ballroom. Important people were there to raise money for a minority golf scholarship. I was the entertainer. Dondré was an eighteen-year-old from Monroe, Louisiana. He was the 5 evening's honored guest.

Dondré attended a mainly white Southern high school. Dondré, a senior, was black.

He stepped up to the microphone. The audience stood and clapped. Then, Dondré said:

10 "I love golf," he said. "For the past two years, I've been a member of the St. Frederick High School golf team. And though I was the only black member, I've always felt at home playing at the mostly white country clubs across Louisiana."

15 Dondré then told us how that feeling changed on April 17, 1991.

"Our team had driven from Monroe. When we arrived at the Caldwell Parish Country Club in Columbia, we walked to the putting green," Dondré said.

20 A man from the club spoke to the team's coach. Then, Coach Murphy returned to his players.

"I want to see the seniors," he said.

"I don't know how to tell you this," Murphy told the four seniors. "But the Caldwell Parish Country Club is reserved for 25 whites only. I want you seniors to decide what our response should be. If we leave, we forfeit[1] the tournament. If we stay, Dondré can't play."

Listening to Dondré's story, I remembered a similar experience.

---

1. **forfeit** (FAWR fuht): to lose or give up something as a penalty.

"A Mason-Dixon Memory" by Clifton Davis, slightly adapted from *Reader's Digest*, March 1993. Copyright © 1993 by Mel White. Retold by Holt, Rinehart and Winston. Reproduced by permission of **Mel White**.

30 In 1959 I was thirteen years old. My mother, my stepfather, and I lived in a small black ghetto in Long Island, New York. Our eighth-grade class was to visit Washington, D.C., and Glen Echo Amusement Park in Maryland.

Because our family was poor, I had to raise money for the
35 trip myself. I sold candy bars, delivered newspapers, and mowed lawns. Three days before the deadline, I had made enough. I was going!

I was the only nonwhite in our part of the train to Washington. At the hotel in D.C., I roomed with Frank Miller,
40 a businessman's son. Together, we dropped water balloons out our hotel window. We soon became close friends.

Every morning, we boarded the school bus for an adventure. We visited the Lincoln Memorial. We read Lincoln's Gettysburg Address. The speech was about the
45 bloodiest fight in the Civil War. It said: ". . . we here highly resolve that these dead shall not have died in vain—that this nation, under God, shall have a new birth of freedom. . . ." Lincoln's face seemed very sad. The next morning, I knew why.

50 "Clifton," a chaperone said, "could I see you?"

My friends turned pale. They thought we'd been caught throwing water balloons.

"Do you know about the Mason-Dixon line?" she asked.
"No," I said.

55 "Before the Civil War," she said, "the Mason-Dixon line was the dividing line between slave states and free states. Today the Mason-Dixon line is an invisible border between the North and the South. Things change when you leave Washington, D.C., and enter Maryland."

60 She then told me that Glen Echo Amusement Park, in Maryland, did not allow Negroes inside.

Here's HOW
FLASHBACK

The writer is an entertainer at an event to raise money for a minority golf scholarship.

The writer listens to a boy's speech, which reminds him of an event from his own childhood.

Flashback: The writer describes something that happened to him in 1959, when he was thirteen years old.

Here's HOW
THE ESSAY

Lines 55–59 are important for this essay because they explain the title. Just because Clifton is black, he's not allowed to go to an amusement park in the South. I think the purpose of this essay is to show us how prejudice is hurtful and stupid. The writer shares his life experience.

Your
TURN

THE ESSAY

Re-read lines 77–82. What emotions does Clifton feel when all eleven of his classmates decide not to go to the amusement park?

_____

_____

_____

What is the author's purpose in sharing these emotions?

_____

_____

_____

_____

Your
TURN

FLASHBACK

In lines 83–87, the flashback ends, and the writer returns to the time when the story started. Underline the sentence that shows us the flashback has ended.

Back in our room, Frank said, "What happened, Clifton? Are we in trouble?"

I just lay on my bed and began to cry. Frank was shocked.
65 Junior-high boys didn't cry too often.

Suddenly, I knew how it felt to be a "nigger." Never before had I been kept out of a place because of my race.

"Clifton," Frank whispered, "what is the matter?"

"They won't let me go to Glen Echo Park tonight because
70 I'm a Negro."

"Phew!" Frank said. "I thought it was serious!"

I stared at him. "It _is_ serious. They don't let Negroes into the park. I can't go with you!" I shouted. "That's pretty serious to me."

75 I was ready to punch Frank in the face. Then he said, "Then I won't go either."

For a minute, we didn't move. Then, Frank grinned. I will never forget that moment. Soon, eleven white boys had joined me in the room. They had all wanted to go to the
80 amusement park. But they all decided, "We won't go." We had started a small revolution. My heart began to race. I was not alone. I felt grateful and proud.

Dondré Green's teammates were like my friends. Standing by their friend cost them a lot. But when it was
85 time to decide, no one stopped to think. "Let's get out of here," one of his teammates whispered. And they left, just like that. Not only the seniors, but the younger players, too.

Dondré was amazed by his friends' response. The people of Louisiana also surprised him. They passed a new law.
90 Now, private groups cannot invite a team and then bar a team member because of race.

As he spoke to us, Dondré's eyes filled with tears. "I love my coach and my teammates for sticking by me," he

said. "It goes to show that there are always good people who
95 will not give in to bigotry.[2] The kind of love they showed me
that day will conquer hatred every time."

Suddenly the banquet crowd was standing and clapping.

In Washington, D.C., my friends showed that kind of love.
A chaperone appeared with tickets to a Senators-Tigers
100 game. Everyone cheered. We'd never been to a professional
baseball game before.

On the way to the game, we stopped by the Lincoln
Memorial. Everyone grew silent. I stared at Mr. Lincoln. His
eyes still looked sad and tired.

105 I remembered the words of his speech: ". . . we here
highly resolve . . . that this nation, under God, shall have a
new birth of freedom. . . ."

Lincoln's words were telling us that freedom is not free.
Everyone should be let into amusement parks and
110 country clubs. When they are not, the war for freedom
begins again. Sometimes the war is fought with fists and
guns. More often the best weapon is a simple act of love
and courage.

Lincoln's words always remind me of my eleven white
115 friends. I like to think that when we stopped that night, Mr.
Lincoln smiled at last. As Dondré said, "The kind of love they
showed me that day will conquer hatred every time."

Here's HOW

FLASHBACK

In lines 98–107, the story returns to the flashback. The writer shows that it is a flashback by saying "In Washington, D.C." Since that is where the flashback took place, I know the flashback has begun again.

Your TURN

THE ESSAY

Re-read lines 109–111. In your opinion, which of the two sentences contains the main idea of this essay? Underline the sentence, and explain your answer below.

_____

_____

_____

_____

_____

_____

---

2. bigotry (BIHG uh tree): hatred toward people who are different in race, religion, politics, or other beliefs.

Text Structures: Flashbacks

Essays, like other pieces of writing, are structured to help make their meaning clear. The essay you just read is structured around **flashbacks.** The writer twice goes back to an earlier time to tell a story that relates to the first story he is telling.

Think about the writer's purpose in using flashbacks in "A Mason-Dixon Memory." How were the experiences of Dondré Green and Clifton Davis alike? Fill in the chart below. First, describe Green's experience and his friends' response. Then, describe Davis's experience and his friends' response. Finally, explain the main idea of the essay. Part of the chart has been completed for you.

	Experience	Friends' Response
Dondré Green (1991)	_____ _____ _____ _____	They stand by their friend. They decide they won't play at the golf club, either. Even the younger players leave.
Clifton Davis (1959)	_____ _____ _____ _____	_____ _____ _____ _____

What is the **main idea** of the essay?

_____
_____
_____
_____

Vocabulary

A. Match words and definitions. Write the letter of the correct definition on the line next to each word. The first one has been done for you.

_____e_____ **1.** putting green   **a.** narrow-minded behavior

_____ **2.** ghetto   **b.** a person who goes with and is responsible for a group of young people

_____ **3.** resolve   **c.** a part of a city in which a minority group lives

_____ **4.** bigotry   **d.** to declare in a formal manner

_____ **5.** chaperone   **e.** in golf, an area of closely mowed grass in which the hole is sunk

B. Choose two words from the above list. Use each word in a sentence.

1. _____

_____

_____

_____

2. _____

_____

_____

_____

Buddies Bare Their Affection
for Ill Classmate

Reading Skill: Summarizing

A **summary** restates the main events or main ideas of a story in a shorter form than the original story. Summarizing (summary writing) is useful because it can help you remember the most important ideas in a story you've just read.

Before you write a summary, read the story carefully. Decide what main ideas and main events are important enough to include in the summary.

You may find it helpful to make a note card for each main event. Every time you finish a part that seems to have a main event, write it on a card like this:

Main Event 1

A fifth-grader has cancer.

Main Event 2

Into the Article

This article is about a fifth-grader who is sick with cancer. The treatment for his cancer causes all his hair to fall out. His friends don't want him to stand out because of his bald head, so they do something very nice for him.

1 **O**ceanside, California, March 19 — In Mr. Alter's class, nearly all the boys are bald. Thirteen fifth-graders shaved their heads for a sick buddy. They didn't want him to feel different.

5 Eleven-year-old Scott Sebelius explained. "People can't tell who's who. They don't know who has cancer."

Ian O'Gorman is the one with cancer. His disease is called lymphoma. First, doctors removed a tumor. Then, he started chemotherapy.[1]

10 "I had tubes up my nose," Ian said. "And I had butterflies in my stomach."

Ian has eight more weeks of chemotherapy. It will make all his hair fall out. Before that happens, he chose to shave his head. His friends astonished[2] him by shaving theirs, too.

15 It was ten-year-old Kyle Hanslik's idea. All the boys went to the barbershop together.

Ian's father choked back tears. He is moved by the boys' support. Jim Alter, Ian's teacher, shaved his head, too.

20 On March 2 Ian left the hospital. He is pale and twenty pounds lighter. But he's eager to play baseball and basketball. He thinks he can start on Monday.

—from the *Austin American-Statesman*

Here's HOW

SUMMARIZING

The main idea of lines 1–4 is that a group of fifth-graders shaved their heads because a classmate is sick. That's a main idea I will need to have in my summary.

Your TURN

SUMMARIZING

What is the main idea of lines 7–9? Write your answer on the lines below.

_____

_____

_____

_____

_____

_____

_____

_____

_____

_____

_____

_____

---

1. **chemotherapy** (KEE moh THEHR uh pee): the use of chemical agents to treat disease.
2. **astonished** (uh STAHN ihsht): to be suddenly surprised.

"Buddies Bare Their Affection for Ill Classmate" adapted from *Austin American-Statesman*, March 19, 1994. Copyright © 1994 by The Associated Press. Retold by Holt, Rinehart and Winston. Reprinted by permission of **The Associated Press.**

Summarizing

The graphic organizer below can be used to collect information for your summary. Fill in the boxes as you read the newspaper article "Buddies Bare Affection for Ill Classmate." The first box has been done for you.

Main Events

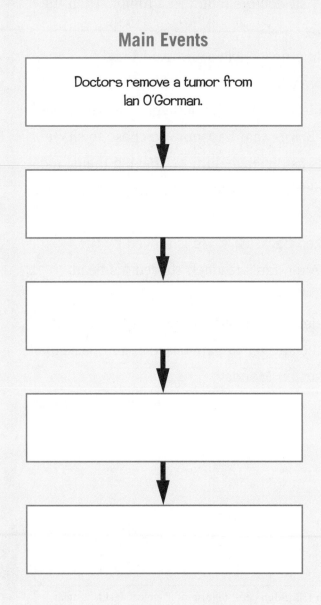

Doctors remove a tumor from Ian O'Gorman.

Summarizing

Use the information in the boxes on the previous page to write a summary paragraph.

Summary

_____

_____

_____

_____

_____

_____

_____

_____

_____

The Origin of the Seasons

Literary Focus: Origin Myths

How did the earth come to be? Why is there night and day? Why do the seasons change? Ancient people turned to their mythmakers to answer these questions. The mythmakers gave explanations of how the world works. **Origin myths** are the special type of myths that explain how something was created or came to be.

Reading Focus: Cause and Effect

Since origin myths explain how something came to be, they tell about causes and their effects. A **cause** makes something happen. What happens is called an **effect.** In origin myths, often the gods do something that causes an effect on earth. The earth reacts to what the gods do. That reaction, in turn, has another effect on the gods, and so on. This type of pattern is called a **cause-and-effect chain.**

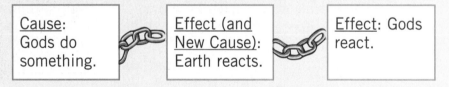

Cause: Gods do something. → Effect (and New Cause): Earth reacts. → Effect: Gods react.

Into the Myth

Do you have four distinct seasons where you come from? Or do you live in a region where the weather rarely changes? Which of those situations do you think is better? As you read this myth, think about whether the seasons are a reward or a punishment.

The Origin of the Seasons

BASED ON THE MYTH RETOLD BY
Olivia Coolidge

Cast of Characters

Demeter (dih MEE tuhr): Goddess of the harvest.

Persephone (puhr SEHF uh nee): Demeter's daughter.

Hades (HAY deez): God of the dead.

Zeus (zoos): The chief god.

Phoebus (FEE buhs) **Apollo**: God of the sun.

Demeter was the great earth mother. She stood tall. Her hair was the color of wheat. She was the goddess of the harvest[1] and taught the farmers everything they knew. Demeter's daughter was named Persephone.

5   Persephone was the young girl of spring. She lived in a land where the spring is long and lovely. There she played and laughed with other girls. One day Hades heard Persephone's laughter. Hades was the god of the dead, but even he was touched by Persephone's beauty. He wanted to

10   marry her. So, Hades went up to Olympus to get permission from Zeus, the chief god. Zeus agreed that Hades could take Persephone as his wife.

One day Persephone was gathering flowers with her friends. Persephone wandered away from the other girls. As

15   she looked a little ahead, she noticed the most beautiful flower. She stretched out her hand to reach for the flower. Suddenly, the earth opened in front of her. Then, she found herself caught in a stranger's arms. Persephone screamed and tried to get free. Her armful of flowers fell to earth. However,

20   Hades was far stronger than she. He swept her into his golden chariot, took the reins of his coal-black horses, and was gone. The earth made a rumbling[2] sound as it closed behind them. The other girls ran to find Persephone. They went to the place where they had seen her last, but they

25   couldn't find her anywhere. All they saw were roses and lilies scattered over the grass.

When Demeter heard the news of her daughter's disappearance, she was overcome with sadness. She searched

---

1. **harvest** (HAHR vihst): the gathering of a food crop.
2. **rumbling** (RUHM buhl ihng): a deep, heavy, continuous sound.

everywhere. She asked everyone she met if they had seen her
30 daughter. Neither gods nor men had seen Persephone.
Demeter finally asked the god Phoebus Apollo. He sees all
things from his chariot in the heavens.

"Yes, I have seen your daughter," said the god. "Hades
has taken her, and Zeus agreed to it."

35 When she heard this, Demeter became very upset. With
Zeus on Hades' side, she knew that she would never be able
to rescue Persephone. Demeter decided to disguise herself as
an old woman and wander the earth.

While she wandered, Demeter forgot all about her duties
40 as the harvest goddess. No fruit, vegetables, or wheat grew
anymore. The gods looked down on the earth. They realized
that people might starve to death unless Demeter helped
things grow again.

At last, Zeus sent Iris, the rainbow, to seek out Demeter.
45 He wanted Iris to ask Demeter to save the people on earth.
Dazzling Iris swept down from Olympus. She offered Demeter
beautiful gifts from the other gods. But Demeter would not
listen. She said that she would not let fruit grow on the earth
until Persephone was returned to her.

50 Finally, Zeus saw that he must send a messenger to bring
back Persephone to her mother. The messenger went to the
land of the dead. He found Hades sitting upon his throne.
Persephone sat pale and sad beside him. She hadn't had
anything to eat or drink since she'd been in the land of the
55 dead. She sprang up with joy when she saw Zeus's
messenger. Hades looked gloomy because he really loved
Persephone. He knew he couldn't disobey Zeus, though. So,
he came up with a trick. He pressed Persephone to eat with
him before she left. Persephone really wanted to get out of
60 there, but Hades begged her to take a pomegranate.
Persephone didn't want to delay her trip by arguing. She

THE ORIGIN OF THE SEASONS   **151**

Here's HOW

ORIGIN MYTH

I just read a myth about Phoebus Apollo (line 31). He's the god who drives a chariot across the sky. The ancient Greeks believed that Apollo's chariot gave light to the world.

Your TURN

CAUSE AND EFFECT

Demeter becomes sad when she hears about what happened to her daughter. What effect does Demeter's sadness have on earth? Circle the paragraph that describes this effect.

Your TURN

CAUSE AND EFFECT

Why does Zeus send a messenger to bring back Persephone?

_____

_____

_____

CAUSE AND EFFECT

I see a cause-and-effect chain in lines 56–64:

Hades wants Persephone to stay (cause).

He offers her food (effect and new cause).

Persephone, in a hurry, eats some of the food (effect).

Your
TURN

CAUSE AND EFFECT

Why does Persephone live in the land of the dead for seven months? Why not four or five months? To find the cause, re-read lines 71–77.

_____

_____

ORIGIN MYTH

This myth explains two seasons: Persephone spends seven months with Hades and five months with her mother. I don't get how this myth explains all four seasons, though. Maybe that's not the purpose of this myth.

thought it would be easier to say yes. So, she ate seven of the pomegranate seeds. Then, Zeus's messenger took her with him. Persephone finally came back to earth.

65   When Demeter saw Zeus's messenger with her daughter, she rushed forward. Persephone, too, rushed forward. She threw her arms around her mother's neck. For a long time, they held each other. But then Demeter asked the girl, "Did you eat or drink anything with Hades?" The girl replied, "I

70 took a pomegranate and ate seven of its seeds."

"Oh, no!" said the goddess. "My daughter, what have you done? The Fates have said that if you ate anything in the land of the dead, you must return to Hades. However, you didn't eat the whole pomegranate. You ate only seven of its seeds.

75 Therefore, you must live in the land of the dead for seven months of the year. For the other five months, you may live with me."

And that's what the Fates decided. Even Zeus could not change their minds. For seven months every year, Persephone

80 lives in the land of the dead. At this time, Demeter is sad and misses her daughter. The trees lose their leaves. The cold comes. The earth lies still and dead. After seven months, Persephone returns. Her mother is glad, and the earth is happy. The wheat springs up. It is bright, fresh, and green in

85 the fields. Flowers bloom, birds sing, and young animals are born. The heavens smile for joy.

Cause-and-Effect Chain

Many events in the ancient myth you just read are connected by **cause and effect.** Look back at the selection to fill out the diagram below. Read each cause, the reason something happened. Then, describe the effect of each cause. Part of the chart has been completed for you.

1. <u>Cause</u>: Hades falls in love with Persephone.

<u>Effect</u>: _____

_____

2. <u>Cause</u>: Demeter is sad about the loss of her daughter.

<u>Effect</u>: _____

_____

3. <u>Cause</u>: Zeus sends Iris, the rainbow, to persuade Demeter to return to her duties as the harvest goddess.

<u>Effect</u>: Demeter says she will not let any fruit grow on the earth until her daughter is returned to her.

4. <u>Cause</u>: Zeus sends a messenger to take Persephone away from Hades.

<u>Effect</u>: _____

_____

5. <u>Cause</u>: Persephone eats seven pomegranate seeds.

<u>Effect</u>: _____

_____

The Flight of Icarus

Literary Focus: Morals of Myths

A **moral** is a lesson about the right way to behave. The
Greeks used morals in many myths to teach children values.
Some common morals are "Look before you leap" and
"Honesty is the best policy."

Reading Skill: Making Generalizations

When you **make a generalization,** you form a general idea
based on the facts and details you read. You make
generalizations all the time in real life. For instance, you
might say, "Many people in my class like games." In this
case, you are making a generalization from your experience
with your classmates.

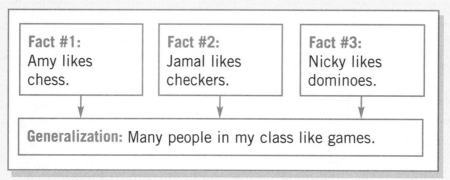

Fact #1: Amy likes chess.	Fact #2: Jamal likes checkers.	Fact #3: Nicky likes dominoes.

Generalization: Many people in my class like games.

When you read, making generalizations is one way to make
sense out of the details in a text.

Into the Myth

This is part of a myth about a great inventor named Daedalus
and his young son, Icarus. Daedalus had built a huge maze for
King Minos. The maze was called the labyrinth (LAB uh
rihnth). Now, King Minos has trapped Daedalus and Icarus.
Daedalus has to invent a way to escape.

The Flight of Icarus

Based on the Myth Retold by
Sally Benson

Cast of Characters

King Minos (MY nuhs): King of Crete.

Theseus (THEE see uhs): Hero from Athens held captive by Minos. Daedalus helped him escape from Crete.

Daedalus (DEH duh luhs): Built the labyrinth for Minos.

Icarus (IH kuh ruhs): Daedalus's young son.

After Theseus escaped, King Minos was angry. He locked Daedalus, the builder of his labyrinth, in a tower. Icarus, Daedalus's young son, helped his father escape.

Because Crete is an island, Daedalus and Icarus were still
5 prisoners. They tried—and failed—to escape by ship.

Daedalus said, "I will try the air." He told Icarus to bring him feathers. Daedalus shaped wax into wings and covered them with the feathers.

When Daedalus tried out the wings, the wind lifted him
10 up. Excitedly, he made a pair of wings for Icarus. Icarus tried them out and was able to fly.

"Now we will escape," said Daedalus. "Don't fly low, or your wings will become wet and heavy. Don't fly high, or the sun will melt the wax."

15 Together they began their flight across the sea.

Icarus loved the freedom of flight. He flew higher, closer and closer to the blazing sun. The wax began to melt—small feathers and then large feathers dropped off. Wildly, Icarus beat his wings, but there were no feathers to hold him up. He
20 plunged into the sea and drowned.

Daedalus gathered his son's body in his arms and flew to land. There he buried Icarus.

Then, Daedalus flew to the island of Sicily where he built a temple for the god Apollo. His wings were hung in the
25 temple as a gift to the god. Daedalus mourned for Icarus, who had not listened to his father's words and had flown too close to the sun.

"The Flight of Icarus" adapted from *Stories of the Gods and Heroes* by Sally Benson. Copyright 1940 and renewed © 1968 by Sally Benson. All rights reserved. Retold by Holt, Rinehart and Winston. Reproduced by permission of **Dial Books for Young Readers, a division of Penguin Young Readers Group, a Member of Penguin Group (USA) Inc., 345 Hudson St., New York NY 10014.**

Morals of Myths: Story Map

The elements of a story or myth can be charted in a **story map** like the one below. Use the first five boxes to list the main parts of the **plot** of "The Flight of Icarus." Then, review the information and try to state the **moral,** or message, of the myth. Part of the chart has been filled in for you.

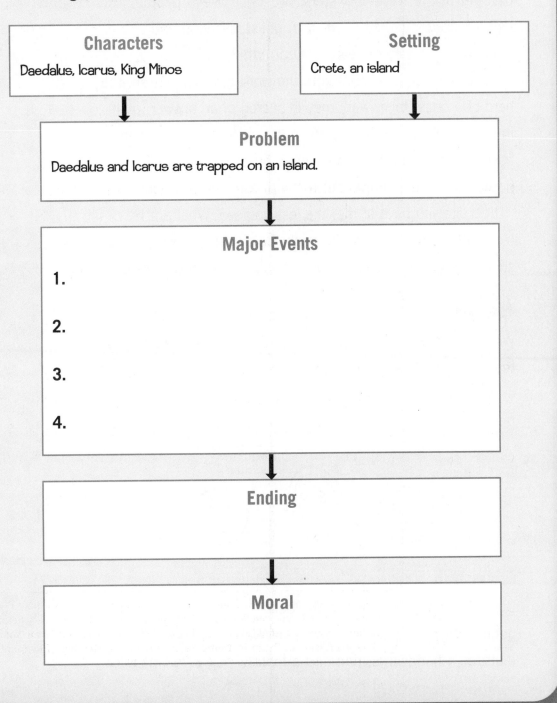

Characters

Daedalus, Icarus, King Minos

Setting

Crete, an island

Problem

Daedalus and Icarus are trapped on an island.

Major Events

1.

2.

3.

4.

Ending

Moral

Sir Gawain and the Loathly Lady

Literary Focus: The Quest

You probably know this story: A person leaves home to look for a treasure. Along the way, the person faces many things that get in the way—monsters, dragons, or evil people. This type of story is called a *quest*. A **quest** is a long and dangerous journey in search of something valuable.

The word *quest* is related to the word *question*. Often, the hero of a quest takes a journey in search of an answer to an important question. For instance, the hero of a quest might have to answer a **riddle**—a puzzling question or problem. A riddle might be a simple but tricky question such as this one: "The more you have of me, the less you see. What am I?" (Answer: Darkness!) A riddle might be a much larger question such as this one: "What do women want most in the world?"

Reading Skill: Reading Aloud/Fluency

What should you do if you can't understand a passage you're reading? Here's a tip: Read the passage aloud several times, or have someone else read it aloud to you. Listening to a passage can help you understand it better.

Into the Legend

Does the term "beauty and the beast" make you think of a beautiful woman and an ugly man? Well, this legend features a handsome man and a loathly—ugly—woman.

Sir Gawain and the Loathly Lady

BASED ON THE LEGEND RETOLD BY
Betsy Hearne

The Granger Collection, New York

One day in spring, King Arthur was hunting with all his knights. Suddenly a deer ran by in the distance. King Arthur told his knights that he would chase the deer by himself. King Arthur went after the deer until he killed it. He was

5 about to call for his knights when he heard a voice behind him.

"Well done, King Arthur!"

King Arthur turned to see a strange knight. The knight was fully armed. He was standing only a few yards away.

10 "You have done me wrong many years and given away my northern lands," said the strange knight. "I have your life in my hands. What will you do now?"

"Sir Knight, what is your name?" asked the king.

"My name is Gromer Somer Joure."

15 "Spare my life, Sir Gromer, and I'll give you whatever I can. It is shameful to kill me here. I have only my hunting gear, but you're armed for battle."

"I'll spare your life if you promise me something. You will meet me here on this day one year from now. None of your

20 knights will come with you. On that day, you must tell me the answer to this riddle: What do women want? If you do not bring the answer to my riddle, you will lose your head."

"I promise," said the king. "Now let me go."

The knight laughed. "Do not think of playing false, King

25 Arthur."

"I won't. I'm a true knight." The king began to blow his bugle[1] for his knights to find him. Sir Gromer turned his

---

1. **bugle** (BYOO guhl): a musical instrument made of brass or copper, like a small trumpet.

"Sir Gawain and the Loathly Lady" adapted from *The Oryx Multicultural Folktale Series: Beauties and Beasts* by Betsy Hearne. Copyright © 1993 by The Oryx Press. Retold by Holt, Rinehart and Winston. Reproduced by permission of **Greenwood Publishing Group, Inc.,** Westport, CT for Oryx Press.

horse and was gone as quickly as he had come. The knights found their king alone with the deer he had killed.

30 The king told his favorite knight, Sir Gawain, what had happened.

"Don't worry," said Gawain. "Get your horse ready to ride into strange country. Ask everyone you meet the answer to the riddle. I will ride another way, and I will write all the
35 answers in a book."

So, Gawain rode one way, and the king another. Each one asked every man and woman he found, "What do women want?"

Some said women loved beautiful clothes. Some said they
40 loved to be praised. Some said they loved a handsome man. Some said one thing, and others said another. Gawain had so many answers that he made a great book to hold them. After many months of traveling, he came back to King Arthur's court. The king was there already with his book. Each looked
45 over the other's work. But no answer seemed right.

King Arthur decided that he needed to look a little more. He had only a month left. So, he rode away to Ingleswood Forest.

There he met a lady. King Arthur was amazed. She was
50 the ugliest creature that he had ever seen. Her face seemed almost like that of an animal. She had a pushed-in nose and a few yellow teeth in her mouth. Her body was twisted. She had a hunched back. But she rode cheerfully on her horse. Her voice was sweet and soft.

55 "I am glad that I have met with you, King Arthur," Dame Ragnell said. "Speak with me. Your life is in my hands. I know of your situation. I warn you that you will not find your answer if I do not tell you."

"What do you want with me, lady?" said the king. He was
60 surprised that she was so bold.

Here's HOW

THE QUEST

There's Gawain! In line 30, I find out that Gawain is King Arthur's favorite knight. Gawain must be very special. He's going to help King Arthur in his quest to find the answer to the riddle.

Your TURN

THE QUEST

How do King Arthur and Sir Gawain plan to find the answer to the riddle? Do you think this is a good plan? Explain.

_____

_____

_____

_____

_____

Your TURN

READING ALOUD

Re-read lines 49–58, and circle the description of Dame Ragnell's voice. Now, read aloud what Dame Ragnell says to King Arthur. (text in box) If you want to be theatrical, pretend you look like Dame Ragnell while you read her lines.

THE QUEST

King Arthur was forced to make a deal with Sir Gromer. Now, in his quest to find the answer to the riddle, King Arthur is again presented with a deal. Reread lines 61–66. What choice does King Arthur face now? What is his answer?

_____

_____

_____

_____

_____

THE QUEST

Circle the answer to the riddle in lines 91–92. Do you think this is a good answer? Why or why not?

_____

_____

_____

_____

_____

"I will make you a deal," said Dame Ragnell slowly. "If your life is saved another way, you don't need to grant my wish. If my answer saves your life, grant me Sir Gawain as my husband. Choose now."

65   "I cannot grant you Sir Gawain," said the king. "That's his choice. He is not mine to give."

"Well," she said, "then go home again and speak to Sir Gawain. Even though I'm ugly, I'm in good spirits. Through me, he may save your life."

70   They said goodbye to each other. The king returned to Carlyle with a heavy heart. The first man he met was Sir Gawain. "How did it go?" Gawain asked.

"Couldn't be worse," said the king. "I'm afraid that I'll die at Sir Gromer's hand."

75   "No," said Gawain. "I would rather die myself. I will do anything to help you."

"Gawain, I met today with the ugliest lady that I have ever seen. She said she would save my life if you became her husband."

80   "Is that all?" asked Gawain. "Then I shall marry her and marry her again! I don't care if she's as ugly as the devil. You are my king, and I am your friend. It is my duty to save your life. If I don't, I'm a big coward."

"Thank you, Gawain," said King Arthur. "You have saved
85 my life."

The day soon came when the king was to meet Dame Ragnell and take his answer to Sir Gromer. The king rode about a mile when he met Dame Ragnell. He told her that Gawain had agreed to marry her.

90   "Now you will know the answer to your riddle," began Dame Ragnell. "There is one thing that every woman wants: We want to rule over men. Then, all is ours. Now go and tell that to your knight. You will not be harmed."

The king went off to meet Sir Gromer and tell him the

95 answer to the riddle.

When he heard King Arthur's answer, Sir Gromer was silent. He was angry. Then he cried out, "I hope to God that the one who told you the answer will burn in a fire. She's my sister, Dame Ragnell. She wasted my time. Go where you like,

100 King Arthur."

Now King Arthur had to follow through with his promise to Dame Ragnell. He was ashamed to bring the ugly lady to the court. When they arrived at Carlyle, everyone wondered where she came from. They had never seen such an ugly

105 creature.

When he saw the king and Dame Ragnell coming, Sir Gawain stepped forward and said, "I am ready to follow through with my promise."

"God have mercy," said Dame Ragnell when she saw

110 Gawain. "For your sake I wish I were a pretty woman because you're such a good person."

At the wedding, Dame Ragnell dressed better than anyone else. But all her fine clothes could not hide her ugliness. When the party began, only Dame Ragnell ate with an

115 appetite. All the other ladies and gentlemen sat like stones. After the wedding party, Sir Gawain and Lady Ragnell went to the bedroom that had been prepared for them.

"Ah, Gawain," said the lady. "Since we are married, be polite and come to bed. If I were pretty, you would be happy.

120 For Arthur's sake, kiss me at least."

Sir Gawain turned to the lady. But instead of the ugly lady, he saw the loveliest lady he had ever seen.

"What are you?" cried Gawain.

"Sir, I am your wife, of course. Why are you so mean?"

125 "Lady, I am sorry," said Gawain. "Now you are a beautiful lady, and today you were the ugliest woman that I've ever

Here's HOW

THE QUEST

In quest stories, there's usually a villain who gets in the way of the hero. Sir Gromer is a villain, but he still acts like a knight. When King Arthur gives him the correct answer, Sir Gromer keeps to his part of the deal. He doesn't kill the king. A knight's word of honor is important.

Your TURN

READ ALOUD

Read aloud the dialogue between Dame Ragnell and Sir Gawain in lines 107–111. Make sure you change your voice to play each character!

Your TURN

THE QUEST

What happens to Dame Ragnell? Why do you think this happens?

_____

_____

_____

The Granger Collection, New York

Your
TURN

THE QUEST

Re-read lines 129–132
Circle the important choice
Dame Ragnell presents to
Sir Gawain. How does
Gawain repond?

_____

_____

_____

_____

How is this response
related to the answer to the
riddle Dame Ragnell gave
(lines 91–92)?

_____

_____

_____

_____

_____

Your
TURN

READING ALOUD

Read aloud the last two
paragraphs of the story.
Circle the name of the
character who speaks last.

seen." And he took her in his arms and kissed her with great
joy.

"Sir," she said, "you have half-broken the spell on me. So,
130 you will have me, but my beauty won't stay. You may see me
pretty by night and ugly by day, or else see me ugly by night
and pretty by day.

"The choice is too hard!" cried Gawain. "I don't know
what I should say. The choice is in your hands!"

135 "Thank you, Gawain," said the lady. "Now I know I am
truly loved. I can be pretty for you both day and night. I was
shaped by witchcraft by my stepmother. According to her
spell, I was to be the ugliest creature until the best knight of
England married me and let me have control. Kiss me, Sir
140 Gawain. Be happy." The two thanked God for their good
fortune.

King Arthur came himself to call them to breakfast the
next day. He wondered why Gawain stayed so late with his
ugly bride. Sir Gawain rose and took the hand of the lady. He
145 opened the door to greet the king.

Dame Ragnell stood by the fire, with her pale, lovely skin
and red hair, which spilled down to her knees. "Look," said
Gawain to the king, "this is my wife, Dame Ragnell. She once
saved your life." And Gawain told the king about the
150 stepmother's spell.

From then on, Dame Ragnell was always the prettiest lady
at every party. Sir Gawain loved her all his life.

The Quest: Decision Making

A **quest** is a long journey in search of something valuable, such as a treasure, a kingdom, or the hand of a beautiful maiden. Along the way, the hero usually faces important choices. The success of the quest depends on the hero's **decision-making** abilities.

In the legend you just read, King Arthur faces many life-or-death choices. At the end of the legend, Sir Gawain, too, has to make a very important choice. The heroes always end up making the right decision. Chart their decision-making processes in the chart below. In the boxes on the left, explain the choice the hero faces. In the box on the right, describe the decision he makes. Part of the chart has been filled in for you.

Either King Arthur agrees to find the answer to the riddle.

Or _____

→ **Decision #1:**

Either King Arthur can go to Gromer with the answers he and Gawain collected.

Or _____

→ **Decision #2:**

Either _____

Or _____

→ **Decision #3:** King Arthur doesn't choose either of these options directly. He says that Gawain is not his to give away. He'll have to ask Gawain if he'll agree to marry Dame Ragnell.

Either Sir Gawain _____

Or _____

→ **Decision #4:**

Letter from Casting Director

Reading Focus: Workplace Documents

In the next fifty years, you will probably hold a variety of jobs. For example, you might be an actor, or you might work for a big corporation. Whatever your job is, you will have to read for information. Documents you need to read for your job are called **workplace documents.**

One type of workplace document is a *business letter.* A **business letter** follows the following pattern.

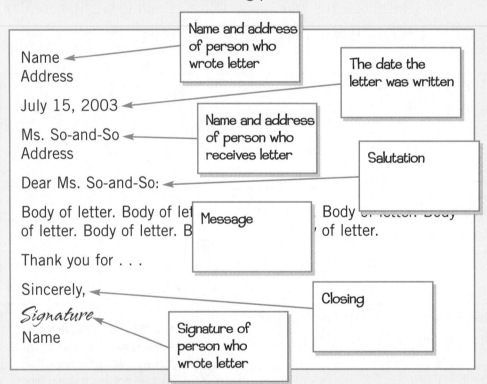

Into the Business Letter

Sam is going to be in a movie! Filming—making the movie—starts soon. Sam receives the business letter shown on the next page. The letter is from the person in charge of hiring actors and actresses. Help Sam figure out what rules she needs to follow on the job.

StreetWheelie Productions
2323 South Robertson Boulevard
Beverly Hills, CA 90210

June 7, 2004

5 Miss Samantha Lancaster
1920 Ygnacio Valley Road
Walnut Creek, CA 94598

Dear Sam:

We at StreetWheelie Productions are pleased to offer you a
10 part in our production. Your contract[1] is included with this
letter. I know that contracts can be difficult to read. So, it is
important that you and your parents understand this
contract completely. Then, you should sign it. We have
listed the issues below.

15 Your Responsibilities
- Transportation: You are responsible for getting to and from
  work.
- Work Schedule: You are responsible for keeping track of
  the filming schedule. Check your e-mail for updates.
20 • Arrival Time: You must arrive on time for work. You
  should report to the makeup person[2] one hour before you
  are supposed to start filming.
- Appearance: You may not change your hairstyle or hair
  color during filming.
25 • Equipment: You must bring your own bike to filming.

---

1. contract (KON trakt): a legal agreement. Contracts can be hard to understand
   unless you're a lawyer. The purpose of this letter is to explain Sam's work
   contract.
2. makeup person: The person who applies makeup (cosmetics) to the actors and
   actresses to help them look the part they're playing.

WORKPLACE DOCUMENT

I can tell this is a business letter by the format. It's from someone at StreetWheelie Productions (lines 1–3). It's written to Samantha Lancaster (line 5).

WORKPLACE DOCUMENT

Lines 20–22 explain Sam's responsibilities—what she has to do for the job.

WORKPLACE DOCUMENT

Re-read lines 20–22. Where should Sam go as soon as she gets to work?

- Parental Supervision:[3] A parent must be present during filming.

Wages

- You will be paid a minimum hourly wage.

30
- You will receive a check at the end of each week.

- You are not allowed to work more than eight hours a day.

- You can take a one-hour break each day. You will get paid for this break.

Bonus

35
- You will receive a bonus (extra money) on the last day of work.

- You will receive this extra money only if you did a good job. You must fulfill all your responsibilities.

- This bonus will equal the total amount you made during

40
the filming. In other words, this bonus will double your money.

If you have any questions, call Juanita Diaz, our lawyer. Her phone number is on the contract. We look forward to having you on the project.

45 Sincerely,

Cassandra Rice

Cassandra Rice, Casting Director

---

3. supervision: watching over, management.

Workplace Documents

Sam thinks, "Wow! I'm going to be in a movie!" Before she knows it, her first day of work arrives. When Sam gets to the location, she receives a list of **workplace instructions.** This document lists all the rules for the job. Making movies is fun, but it's also a business!

Uh-oh. Someone spilled coffee on the workplace instructions. Some of the rules are new to Sam, but most were mentioned in the letter from the casting director. Luckily, you and Sam read that **business letter** very carefully. Look back at the letter, and help Sam write in the parts of items 2 through 4 that are missing in the workplace instructions below.

Talent Instructions:
On Location

1. Arrive on time.

2. When you arrive

3. You may not

4. You must bring you

5. Leave all your personal belongings in your locker.

6. You may talk in nonfilming areas, but there is *no talking* on the filming site.

AUTHOR AND TITLE INDEX